Context
Starter

Workbook
Language, Skills and Exam Trainer
Answer Key & Transcripts

Cornelsen

Chapter 1 | Exercises 1–5

The Answer Key *allows you to check your answers in the case of the controlled exercises where there is a 'right' and a 'wrong' answer. For the more creative exercises you will find a suggested answer, but yours may be different.*
The Answer Key *also contains transcripts of the listening texts.*

1 The Time of Your Life

1 Describing someone's life

a *(Various answers are possible here, for example:)*
In my spare time I go hiking with a couple of friends. We've been all over Germany and have also been in France and the Czech Republic. At work I'm involved in working in a team – I like teamwork – developing new products for the company. I enjoy exploring new places and interacting with others. There's also the thrill of creating new products which will help people in their everyday lives. I had to study for many years to acquire the knowledge and skills for this, but it was worth it.

b *(Various answers are possible here, for example:)*
As my first priority I would choose personal happiness because, without, it success at work or in your hobbies has little value. I agreed with the group that working in a team was important as it gave you support at work, so that's my second priority. Thirdly I feel that security is important.

Key to 'Words in Context' wordlist on pp. 42–43

2 Which words, which phrases?
1 gain acceptance
2 been exposed to … influences
3 peer pressure
4 stage of life
5 has … rights and responsibilities
6 take risks – reach your personal goals
7 play an active role
8 period of transition

3 Saying it, spelling it
a 1 assert
2 rebel
3 conform
4 yearn
5 experiment
6 self-confident
7 provocative

b 1 rebel
2 experimentation
3 confidential
4 provocation

4 What do you call … ?
1 peer group
2 role model
3 coming of age
4 giving serious consideration to your future
5 under pressure
6 popularity

5 Listening comprehension:
Work to live or live to work?

starwb-02: audio transcript
Kerry: Hallo, Phil. Thanks for joining us.
Phil: My pleasure.
Kerry: So, do you agree that working to live seems to be creeping back onto the agenda?
Phil: I think it's certainly a phenomenon that's come back over the last couple of years as we've seen tough economic times in the market place. Erm, you know, graduates in 2008, when that piece was written, just before everything melted down, really were looking for, you know, a lot of different things from the work place. They were looking for some fulfilment, satisfaction, enjoyment. They were looking for the ability to take control of jobs early on rather than having to do years of grunt work before actually getting something interesting to do. And it's amazing how quickly the world changes, when the economy tightens up, two or three years later, 30% or 40% of all graduates were struggling to find work at all, anywhere, and it was a tough market place, so I think that definitely forces people to look at their values and think about what's most important to them.

Kerry: Yes. I think ... I'm going to put a link to this piece in the ... It's just for a bit of nostalgia, maybe. It's quite an interesting read, but the piece was also saying that people sort of looked at their parents' working lives, where they'd perhaps, you know, been working really long hours and they were always kind of chasing a pay cheque, for as big a pay cheque as possible. Do you think this is going to be kind of a cyclical thing, and we've got this trend now where people are going to be chasing a high salary, but then that's going to drop off again.

Phil: I mean, I think it was a phenomenon that took place primarily with the graduates. It's interesting that at Escape the City we tend to work mostly with job changers who are then going into their first or second job, so in their mid-20s through their kind of mid-30s, and we're seeing a very different phenomenon, that we're actually getting people who've been through the graduate programmes and spend three, five ten years working in the big corporates who are now looking at different things from work, beyond just the pay cheque. They're looking for, you know, creating, doing something really interesting and worthwhile. They're looking for enjoyment. They're looking to make a difference in the world. And you know, Dom and Rob started at Escape the City about 18 months ago. They already have 36,000 subscribers, so it's obviously a popular idea, you know, among the next generation ahead from the one that's just going into the workplace now.

Kerry: So, do you think there's a problem with either ... or ... , living to work or working to live? Is there an ideal? I mean, what about you? Which do you ... ?

Phil: My take on it, from my own experience, and working with hundreds of clients, is that there's no perfect answer to this, and actually, what you've got to look at is your overall quality of life. I've seen a kind of movement of more and more, kind of, young people and people in mid-life. They're saying, actually work can be a contributor to quality of life, and enjoyment and satisfaction, whereas maybe our parents' generation saw it purely as a pay cheque in order to, you know, support themselves, pay the rent, put their kids through education, whatever it was they wanted to do. Now we see people are saying, "Actually, work can add to my enjoyment and quality of life as well. We can find work that makes a difference in the world."

Source: http://careers.theguardian.com/audio/graduate-salary-vs-job-satisfaction

a c: He remains neutral.

b 1a, 2b, 3b
    4 He thinks that they see work as part of the quality of life, which contributes to their enjoyment. It's no longer just a way of paying the rent or supporting yourself.

6 **Health and illness**
1 patient
2 blood pressure
3 crutches
4 lower back
5 injuries – surgeon(s)
6 intensive care
7 rehab

7 **About Dave and Jenny**
2 Dave has spent months in hospital since he had the accident.
3 He's walked / been walking on crutches since his leg was amputated.
4 He's had a passion for medicine since he was at elementary school.
5 Since the nurse took Jenny's crutches away, she's been able to walk on her own.
6 Since she discussed the options with her doctors, she's decided to study medicine.
7 Since she talked to her doctors, she's had a better idea of the difficulties.

8 **Playing with sounds and letters**
a 1 an awesome experience
2 they feel under pressure
3 they seek acceptance
4 play an active role
5 a bag of chips
6 it caused an explosion
7 he gazed into her eyes
8 I caught a cab in town

b He meant 'catch-up strategy'; he pronounced 'catch-up' like 'ketchup'.

Chapter 1 | Exercises 9–13

c
1 con<u>tin</u>ue – continu<u>i</u>ty
2 <u>cu</u>rious – curi<u>o</u>sity
3 <u>mys</u>tery – myst<u>e</u>rious
4 <u>op</u>timist – optim<u>i</u>stic
5 <u>per</u>son – person<u>a</u>lity
6 <u>trau</u>ma – trau<u>ma</u>tic
7 un<u>hap</u>py – un<u>ne</u>cessary – un<u>frien</u>dly – un<u>in</u>jured – un<u>in</u>formed – un<u>in</u>teresting
8 The stress is on the main part of the word, not on the prefix.

9 Greater awareness: gerunds and infinitives

a 1b, 2c, 3b, 4b, 5a, 6c, 7a, 8c

b
1	to say	7	choosing
2	to be	8	being
3	seeing	9	reading
4	changing	10	working
5	to study	11	to find
6	to avoid	12	of getting

10 Greater awareness: images in a text

a
1 Movie magazines were <u>her Bible</u>.
2 She studied [movie magazines] <u>with the zealousness of a doctor of divinity</u>.
3 Time was running out <u>like the popcorn at a Clark Gable picture</u>.
4 [She sat] reading movie magazines <u>with her eyes wide as saucers</u>.
5 [The old people's] suitcase was <u>like a burned-out light bulb</u>.
6 [She] could have rented herself out <u>as an earthquake beet</u>.

b (Various answers are possible here, for example:)
'Movie magazines were her Bible' is a metaphor meaning that they had great authority for her, i.e. she took them very seriously, just as devout Christians do the Bible. The simile comparing the suitcase to a burned-out light bulb implies that it was as old and useless as an old light bulb. 'She could have rented herself out as an earthquake beet' refers to the colour of a beetroot – dark red – and the shaking effects of an earthquake. She was blushing and shaking so much because she was very nervous.

11 Creating an outline

Main idea 1: Why people need dreams
a dreams provide people with strength
b dreams give people a goal to aim for

Main idea 2: How Hollywood uses people's dreams
a Hollywood enables people to escape from their everyday lives
b people identify with the characters in the film
c Hollywood films broaden people's horizons

Main idea 3: Positive and negative effects
a films motivate people, giving them a model to look up to and follow
b films mislead people because movie plots are often unrealistic

12 Using a bilingual dictionary

1 It says that *own* is not used with the article. You need to say 'a house of your own' or 'your own house'.
2 our generation – this generation
3 b: Of course, being sensible is a virtue.
   c: Of course, common sense is a virtue.
4 b: Choose a more general word so that it refers to anybody leaving school, e.g. *school leavers*.
   c: Use a less specific word, e.g. *students*.
   I think b or c are correct, because they're more general.
5 *emotions*: I'd choose *emotions* because that's the basic meaning in this context.
6 It gives *brave* and *courageous* and explains that the first is used in dangerous situations, the second when referring to moral decisions, as is the case here.

13 Reporting what people say

a (Various answers are possible here, for example:)
Brian <u>said</u> that he <u>wanted</u> to become a lawyer. Layla <u>told them</u> that her ambition <u>was</u> to become a vet. She <u>added</u> that she <u>loved</u> looking after animals.
Geoff <u>explained/told them</u> that he <u>was thinking</u> of doing Latin and Ancient Greek at uni.
Becky <u>said</u> that she <u>had</u> always <u>wanted</u> to be a journalist, but <u>admitted</u> that now she <u>wasn't</u> so sure.
Andrew <u>explained/told them</u> that he <u>was going</u> to train as a teacher. He <u>explained/added</u> that he <u>thought</u> that teaching kids <u>would be</u> great.

Paula asked Geoff if/whether he really thought it was a good idea to do Classics. She stressed/explained that he might not get a job afterwards. Chris warned Becky to be careful because a lot of newspapers were closing. He suggested/advised trying something else / that she (should) try something else.
Karen asked for (some) advice because she hadn't a clue what to do later.

b (Various answers are possible here, for example:)
Dear Mr Macpherson,
You will probably remember that when I was at Inverness Academy we talked quite a lot about my future plans. Well, recently we had a few people coming to talk to us about the choices open to us after school and one of them made me think, although he didn't tell us much about actual careers. He began by saying that he wanted to talk to us about our future. He said that we might be wondering what a 50-year-old business-man could tell us that would be relevant to our lives. He told us to remember that he had been our age once. He explained that in 1985 he had been working as a young reporter in his home country, South Africa. He added that he'd been/he was a pretty conventional sort of guy from the white suburbs. His life changed dramatically when he met a black girl, Miriam, from one of the townships. Under apartheid it was illegal, but they started going out regularly. His parents and friends were outraged, but he ignored their protests and they were arrested. He lost his job and went through hell, but he stressed that despite all the hardship, he'd never regretted not taking the easy, conventional route. He (had) set up his own computer software business, which was doing well. He's got three kids. He admitted that, like South Africa, the family had had their/its ups and downs, but he and his wife were/are still together. He told us that since apartheid had been abolished, even his parents had gradually come round to accepting his mixed-race family. So he advised us not to be conventional and added that we should follow our heart. He suggested that it would not make our lives easier, but promised us that it would make them more interesting.

14 Giving a short talk
individual answers

15 Difficult choices
a (Various answers are possible here, for example:)
Arthur was the sort of person who liked to have freedom of choice / the freedom to choose / the right to choose [1] between two options. His problem was that he could never make up his mind. When he was faced with an alternative [2], he could never decide in favour [3] of the one option, because that would mean deciding [4] against the other one. He saw the advantages of both and felt that it was wrong to reject [5] any option which had so many good sides to it. So he opted [6] for neither one nor the other. Later, in his thirties, he often complained that freedom was a curse rather than a blessing, but his friends only smiled sadly about a man who had never learned to make a choice [7].

b *individual answers*

Focus on Literature: Narrative Prose – the Novel

1 Gathering information
(Various answers are possible here, for example:)

a Tom Harvey, 16 years old, lives on Crow Lane Estate in South London, seems to have no parents – only mentions his gran; doesn't seem to have many friends ('Alone, but not lonely'), but would like to be better friends with Lucy Walker.

b On his way to the tower block where he and Lucy live, Tom was hit by a mobile phone falling down from the top of that block.

c The accident to his skull may cause Tom to change his personality, maybe he will become obsessed with taking revenge on those who caused it.

2 Looking at language

a *(Various answers are possible here, for example:)*
Kind of OK → all right on the whole ('sort of OK' is possible, but it is also colloquial);
I kind of missed that → I missed that quite a bit;
kind of nice → rather nice

b my gran would babysit for her

c *(Various answers are possible here, for example:)*
Manchmal sah ich sie in der Schule, und gelegentlich gingen wir zusammen nach Hause, und ab und zu ging ich mal zu ihr … , oder sie kam zu mir. (Note: the word 'would' is not apparent in translation!)

3 What's going to happen?

a *(Various answers are possible here, for example:)*
A stretch of grass surrounded by tower blocks, black night, unusually quiet – nothing to be heard except the boy's steps on the frosty grass. The boy is rubbing his icy hands together, you can see his breath misting the cold air. But he walks on steadily with an irresistible sense of purpose. – As he moves on, there is the soft rumble of an idling car engine, and the muffled sound of voices, even laughter. Around the corner a group of hooded gangsters become visible, as well as two large unleashed dogs. The dogs run towards the boy, who now looks almost supernatural with shimmering pale skin radiating light. The dogs move forward to attack him, then suddenly halt and slope off, whimpering quietly.

b *(Various answers are possible here, for example:)*
The atmosphere is icy and dark, i.e. threatening and merciless. The narrator describes himself as being in a 'state of controlled brutality – in control of being out of control', which makes you feel something brutally violent is going to happen. The fact that the dangerous-looking dogs run away from him, scared, gives the impression that he is much more dangerous than any harm they could do. Probably the narrator suspects that the gang members assembled here raped Lucy, so he wants to take revenge on them, maybe with the help of the electric shocks he can cause with his bare hands (see intro). It is clear that there will be a lot of action. It is not clear, however, whether this action will solve the problem Tom is faced with.

2 Communicating in the Digital Age

1 Which is better?

a *(Various answers are possible here, for example:)*

	TV	Internet video platform
advantages	– quality of sound and picture usually better – anonymous: no user profiling	– anyone can upload material – interactive – lots of feedback
disadvantages	– little or no feedback – centralized medium – less variety of content/material	– videos of varying quality – user profiling by Google, e.g. for commercial purposes

b *individual answers*

2 Communicating

a
1. smartphone
2. voiceover IP, e.g. using Skype
3. mobile phone/smartphone
4. instant message/text message
5. social networking site
6. text message/email
7. email
8. speaking face-to-face

b *individual answers*

Key to 'Words in Context' wordlist on pp. 43–45

3 Collocations
1. (going) portable
2. (hand-held) devices
3. access (information)
4. available (online)
5. upload (content to the net)
6. text-based (communication)
7. post (messages)
8. linked (together)

4 Familiar words, familiar phrases?
1. cyberbullies
2. victims
3. enhanced
4. wireless connection – access
5. retrieve
6. social networking sites – false sense of security

5 Crazy collocations

Because so many people now use social networking sites, personal information is becoming widely available to outside sources. What is more, instant messages mean that users can communicate much faster than in the past, which often results in them becoming less careful in their responses. The apparent anonymity of cyberspace also gives them a false sense of security, which may lead some to misuse the new media, e.g. in cyberbullying, since they are unaware of the legal consequences of their actions and think that they can torment their victims without being punished.

6 Cartoons

(Various answers are possible here, for example:)

a The first cartoon shows a mother with a baby in a pushchair (BE)/stroller (AE). The mother is wearing warm clothes because it's snowing. She looks unhappy/depressed. The baby is talking on a mobile phone (BE)/cellphone (AE) and looks happy.
In the second cartoon you can see a couple in the foreground sitting at a table in a restaurant. In the background we (can) see other people in the restaurant using mobile phones. The woman is annoyed at her husband, who seems confused.

b The first cartoon is making fun of the fact that all sorts of people, young and old, use mobile phones in any situation. The second one is making fun of the fact that some people use mobiles to show how important they are, how many friends they've got.

c The first cartoon is pretty effective, because it takes an everyday situation (people using mobiles on the train, for example), and makes it absurd, because a baby doesn't have the ability to use a mobile phone. This absurdity makes it funny.
I don't find the second cartoon so effective because I can't imagine anybody being so truthful about their real motives for using a mobile in public.

7 Structuring a text and connecting ideas

a ☑ There is no clear structure.
☑ There are not enough linking words.
☑ There is no paragraphing.
☐ The writer does not give examples.
☐ The paragraphing is illogical.
☐ The heading does not make sense.

b

Functions	Examples
Organizing the text (listing points)	firstly, secondly, thirdly, another point is, finally
Giving reasons	as, because, since, therefore, thus
Adding ideas	also, besides, in addition, what is more
Comparing thoughts	at the same time, likewise, similarly
Contrasting thoughts	although, but, despite, however, unlike
Giving examples	e.g., for example, such as
Explaining results, consequences	as a result, consequently
Summarizing, drawing conclusions	(finally), in conclusion, in short, to sum up

c (Various answers are possible here, for example:)
Texting can be a good thing because you can communicate with all sorts of people anywhere you like. Unlike calling, you can text several people at once. Texting can also be a very bad thing. One example is when you are at the multiplex and all you hear is people tapping the keys on their phones.
Of course, texting is often useful, since we can communicate with people all over the world. What is more, it is easier than picking up the phone and calling. For example, all we have to do is type 'I love you' to our mums instead of interrupting whatever she is doing by phoning her. Similarly, using your mobile or smartphone is good if you like hearing people's voices, but texting is simpler and is less difficult.
However, texting can be bad, in my opinion, because it may annoy the people around you if you are in a silent place like church or the cinema. Besides, it means that you lose many of the good sides of real communication, such as hearing someone's voice, and it affects family communication as you are too busy texting your friends. The mum who you've just texted to say 'I love you' is the mum you ignore when you're texting. As a result, texting can reduce the time spent on the family.
In short, although texting has its advantages, on the whole, in my view, there are more downsides to it.

8 Listening strategies

starwb-04: audio transcript
SG: OK David hi, I'm Susan, and it's great that we can get together and discuss, I think, a really interesting topic, which is "is the internet bringing out the best in us?" My own view is that if people are spending a lot of time in this new place, this two-dimensional world with just hearing and vision, for every hour they're doing that, that's an hour not being in the real world. Not walking along the beach, giving someone a hug, looking someone in the eye and especially for young people who perhaps haven't rehearsed those skills, those inter-personal skills, and had those three-dimensional experiences where actions have consequences then they might be missing out if they're doing this for long periods of time and as a neuroscientist I'm very aware that the brain adapts to the environment. It's exquisitely evolved, the human brain, to adapt to any environment it's in. So therefore if you have an environment that is so different that perhaps people are existing in for substantial periods of their waking hours, then it's inevitable that the brain will change and my concern is, although there are many good things about the internet, that you can rehearse certain skills, by the same token, there's perhaps certain areas where you might see problems with the tension with possible addiction, with how you use

information, and how that relates to your memory, and above all with how you relate to people, and how you empathise with them.

DB: I mean, it's early days isn't it? And certainly on a kind of neurological level there's a lot of research still to be done. I guess in my experience, say you're looking at using the organisation as a metaphor. With 38 Degrees we're a hyper-connected organisation that relies very heavily on the internet to bring people together and make decisions, we at the same time recognise that there's no substitute for face-to-face contact and so alongside all the online consultations we do with our membership, we also regularly organise curries with members in particular areas because we know that alongside having the conversations on facebook there's a value in sitting down with people and discussing things over beer and poppadums. Maybe the thing we've learned to do is to switch between modes and that seems to be something that a lot of people are fairly able to adapt to. I mean there are, with any new technology you're going to get some people who are antisocial and tweeting when they shouldn't be.

SG: Yeah, of course. The big difference is, these are people you know in real life anyway and then you're communicating via facebook. That's just fine. That's great. That's just fine. When you've never met the people. And, as I say, they're an audience rather than friends, when they're people, you have several hundred of them. And the concern is, the more time you spend doing that, especially for young people, you're not rehearsing those face-to-face skills. You're not rehearsing empathy, you're not rehearsing reading body language, you're not developing in-depth the kind of friendships that people have up until now experienced, simply because you don't have time.

DB: Some of the kind of types of isolation which you're talking about, I think are probably a product as much of economic forces and social change over the last thirty, forty years. I think what we're seeing is actually that in some ways the internet is, at the same time as offering people virtual alternatives to face-to-face contact, it's actually offering people ways of connecting with people, meeting people who are like-minded …

SG: Without doubt.

DB: … And then meeting them in the real world.

SG: Without doubt. And I'd love, for example, my widowed mum who's eighty-five, I'd love her to be on facebook, she refuses, for these very reasons. But I think the problem is, how do we shape an environment, shape a society, where this will happen? I think it's an article of faith. And I know it's nice to be optimistic. I as a scientist, all scientists are optimistic, naturally. How can we get there? Because, I think the trends are – especially with the teenagers – that that's not necessarily the case. That they are, it's such a ready and tempting and non-challenging form of communication where indeed you can not be accountable for what you say. It is very tempting and very exciting and you can communicate all over the world and you can say what you like and people applaud you. You can have lots of followers, you can be cool. How can we help people see that this should be a means to end rather than an end in itself?

DB: My sense is that it's quite hard, right now, to say what the long-term impacts are because some of the things are only very short-term. So we are in the realm of speculation. Which is, it's good to start the debate …

SG: I think that we are dealing with the minds of the next generation. We can't really just sit around, saying that it's been around too short to study, let's give it ten years before we try to do anything or even think about it.

DB: I guess what I'm saying is, the extent to which you act on limited evidence depends on your assessment of risk and I guess my sense is that the picture you're painting is right at the … is quite a long way towards the pessimistic end of the spectrum.

SG: Well, it depends on who you read, and what I personally say is I don't give value judgements but I do say this is something too important to wait. If we look at the literature, if we look at the reports that are coming out, if we look at surveys, if we look at the goods and services that are indicating a certain mind-set of the consumer, then this is something we need to start talking about right now.

http://www.theguardian.com/commentisfree/video/2013/jul/15/internet-susan-greenfield-david-babbs-video-debate

a (*Various answers are possible here, for example:*)
They are likely to be arguing about / discussing whether the internet has changed our lives for the better or not.

b b: One of them is worried about the effects of the internet, the other is more positive.

c (*Various answers are possible here, for example:*)
1 She is a neuroscientist. He is the executive director of a social campaigning site 38 Degrees.
2 She is worried that people who use social networks or the internet a lot do not develop enough face-to-face skills, e.g. empathy, body language and in-depth friendships because they don't have the time to do this.
3 He thinks the internet is not simply an alternative to face-to-face contact. It's also a way of encouraging it.
4 He thinks she's too pessimistic. We don't know what the internet's long-term effects are.

9 How embarrassing!

(*Various answers are possible here, for example:*)
I completely/entirely/perfectly understand why you don't want me to become your 'friend' on your social networking website. It is simply part of your private life. It's important to have privacy, whether you're an adult or a teenager. So I entirely/completely agree with you when you say that you don't want to include me among your 'friends'. It's obvious anyway that as a mother I have a different role than your friends, and I strongly believe in respecting my children's views. They're not necessarily always realistic, because sometimes you react too emotionally, but in this case I think you're perfectly/completely/entirely right – it would be embarrassing to read all your secret/private thoughts, however innocent they may be.

10 Where cyberbullying happens
a It's a bar chart.
b (*Various answers are possible here, for example:*) The most popular venue for cyberbullying, according to the graphic, is instant messaging, where it was experienced by 67% of users. The second most frequently used places for cyberbullying were chat rooms and email, which both accounted for 25% of cases recorded by those interviewed/the interviewees. These were followed by websites and text messages at 23% and 16% respectively.
c The note says that the categories are not mutually exclusive. In other words, people may have experienced cyberbullying in several different places.

11 Modifying the meaning
a 2 I must
3 We were eventually able to
4 You must check
5 You don't have to
6 You should be – what you write may
7 you should remember – may not be – you'll have to

b 1 mustn't: don't have to / needn't
2 could: was able to
3 shall: is said/supposed to
4 mustn't: don't have to / needn't
5 shall: should
6 could: were able to

12 Error spotting
1 'How long have you had your new phone?'
2 'Only for a month. I bought it in May. It was on special offer.'
3 'Oh, how much did it cost?'
4 '£25. I thought that was a bargain.'
5 'I'm looking around at the moment for a new provider. I chose this one because it was cheap, but I often don't get good reception on it and I'm thinking of switching. My old provider was much better, so I may go back to them.'

13 The investigation

(Various answers are possible here, for example:)

Principal: Carson, how long have you known Remy?
Carson: I guess, ever since I joined the school two years ago.
Principal: And when did you start to blackmail her?
Carson: Sir, it wasn't blackmail. I just wanted her help with the magazine I was planning.
Principal: OK, so when did that start?
Carson: Well, sir, I noticed a funny user name on the school website.
Principal: Do you mean this school's website?
Carson: Yes, sir, I mean Clover High School's website. Anyways, I was reading through the messages that YearbookGirl69 had posted / had been posting on the website. I suspected that Remy might be at the back of them, so I decided to test my theory.
Principal: Why was it so important to find out whether Remy was the identity who was hiding behind YearbookGirl69?
Carson: You see, sir, I was having / had been having problems recruiting students to contribute to the magazine, so I thought a little gentle pressure would help to persuade more people to join. Over the weekend I was thinking / had been thinking of ways to persuade her, so I messaged YearbookGirl69 / to test my theory.
Principal: Go on.
Carson: I gave BadBoy2012 as my user name and pasted a picture of Taylor Lautner's abs which I (had) copied off of the Internet.
Principal: And how did she react?
Carson: She took the bait. When I was sitting in the English class the next day, I had a clear view of what she was doing on her computer. I messaged her and saw a window pop up on her PC screen. BadBoy2012 asked YearbookGirl69 what she was wearing, and Remy replied practically nothing. She looked round the class to see if anyone was watching her, but I saw her retrieve a photo from her documents and attach it. After school I went outside and saw her. She was sitting on a bench on her own. I handed her a large envelope with the conversations between BadBoy2012 and YearbookGirl69. Then I took one of the yellow flyers you found and gave it to her.

14 What happened when you were doing that?

(Various answers are possible here, for example:)

1 I was just texting my friend when Mum came home.
2 He was tweeting when suddenly he saw the boss approaching.
3 I was just getting my laptop out of my bag when the phone rang.
4 She was just flopping down on the sofa when she heard Dad's car arrive.
5 They were just comparing their latest smartphones when the teacher came in.
6 I was looking up something on the internet when Dad asked me what I was doing.
7 She was texting a message to her brother when she realized his mobile had been stolen.
8 We were doing research on the internet when Jenny asked me to come to her party.

15 Activities and states

1 prefer
2 are taking up
3 think – remain
4 go
5 are changing
6 fear(s) – are soaring
7 has – tweets
8 were thinking – changed
9 says – seem

16 Nowhere to hide

(Various answers are possible here, for example:)

Erstens kann das Cybermobbing anonym sein, weil der Täter bzw. die Täterin die eigene Identität nicht preisgeben muss. Dies hat zur Folge, dass Täter oder Täterin auch viel radikaler vorgehen kann. Vielfach wird man darin bestärkt, weil es sich nicht um körperliche Gewalt handelt.
Zweitens ist es schwer, Cybermobbing auszuweichen: beim Mobbing ist man zu Hause sicher, während man sich beim Cybermobbing nirgendwo verstecken kann, weil man auch zu Hause per Email oder SMS erreichbar ist.
Drittens gibt es in der Regel keine Überwachung des Cybermobbing, da der Großteil des Cybermobbing durch Emails, SMS und vor allem Instant Messages erfolgt.

Focus on Literature: Narrative Prose – the Short Story

1 How may I help you?
(Various answers are possible here, for example:)
1 Hello, Debbie speaking. (Who's calling?)
2 Is there anything (else) I can do to help you?
3 Thanks for letting me tell you about it / for listening to me.
4 Call me again soon and tell me all about it.

2 What does the narrator tell us?
a 1 Peter: husband/father
  2 Katy: daughter (Can't be wife, because there is the second smile.)
  3 Greta: wife (mother)

b (Various answers are possible here, for example:)
Greta and Katy are travelling somewhere on a train, and Peter has helped them with their suitcase. The last sentence as well as the explanation of Peter's smile for Greta hints at the topic 'husband-wife relationship'.

c 1 narrator: 3rd-person
  2 point of view: probably limited to Greta

Once Peter had brought her suitcase on board the train he seemed eager to get himself out of the way. But not to leave. He explained to her that he was just uneasy that the train should start to move. Out on the platform looking up at their window, he stood waving. Smiling, waving. The smile for Katy was wide open, sunny, without a doubt in the world, as if he believed that she would continue to be a marvel to him, and he to her, forever. The smile for his wife seemed hopeful and trusting, with some sort of determination about it. Something that could not easily be put into words and indeed might never be. If Greta had mentioned such a thing he would have said, Don't be ridiculous. And she would have agreed with him, thinking that it was unnatural for people who saw each other daily, constantly, to have to go through explanations of any kind.

From: "To Reach Japan", in Alice Munro, *Dear Life*. Stories. New York: Vintage Books 2013 (© 2012)

d (Various answers are possible here, for example:)
After I had put Greta's suitcase on board the train, I felt uneasy about staying on the train in case it started moving, so I got down onto the platform but didn't leave of course. Instead, I stood there waving and smiling, especially at little Katy, who is such a marvel to me and always will be. Of course I also smiled at Greta, and she smiled back at me. She is my loving wife and will be back here with me very soon, I'm sure of that.

e (Various answers are possible here, for example:)
Greta's (third-person) point of view shows that she is actually seeing her husband's actions from a kind of distance, which indicates that there might be a problem in their relationship. Peter's first-person narration is more direct, and with fewer hints at future developments.

3 Understanding micro-fiction
1 Wife to husband or husband to wife
2 (Various answers are possible here, for example:)
Speaker: logged on to partner's email and found out about his/her adultery, identified him/her because he or she used their children's names as a password
Partner: obviously wants an extra-marital affair, used their kids' names as a password to the site
3 Sms or twitter

4 Writing a short story
a (Various answers are possible here, for example:)
John was away on business, and I was searching the internet for something or other, when I got bored and suddenly had the idea of logging on to John's email, just for the fun of it. I got a shock when I found a flirtatious email from a strange woman who called herself Pretty Baby alluding to an online dating site. Of course I went to that site immediately to access his user account; I tried out passwords, starting with something I knew we'd both used before, our children's names. Bingo! How disgusting! How could he?

b (Various answers are possible here, for example:)
husband – wife – marriage – adultery – affair – children – future prospects – faithful – loyalty – responsibility – hurt feelings – insult – trust – …

c *individual answers*

3 Living in the Global Village

1 Talking about globalization

1	of	11	from
2	of	12	of
3	to	13	to
4	in	14	over
5	of	15	to
6	in	16	on
7	in/over/during	17	on
8	to	18	in/to
9	of	19	for/on
10	in	20	to

2 Expanding vocabulary

a

Verb	Noun	Adjective
to affect	effect	effective
to apply	application	applicable
to cheapen	cheapness	cheap
to discuss	discussion	—
to exchange	exchange	exchangeable
to explain	explanation	explicable
to fly	flight	—
to mix	mixture/mix	mixable
to save	safety	safe
to subscribe	subscription	—

b *individual answers*

Key to 'Words in Context' wordlist on pp. 45–46

3 What do you call … ?

1. to outsource the production
2. deforestation
3. consumers
4. (large) multinational corporations / (global players)
5. wages
6. depletion
7. pollution
8. to rely on sb.

4 Crossword

a

(crossword grid with answer 15 across: INTERDEPENDENT)

b *individual answers*

Part A: Global citizens

5 An exchange of views

(Various answers are possible here, for example:)

Father: Kannst du Tariq mal fragen, was seine Eltern beruflich machen?

You: Ja klar. Tariq, my dad wants to know what your parents do. Where do they work?

Tariq: Well, my dad's an executive in a cotton mill. And my mum's got a part-time job at a call centre which belongs to a big UK bank.

You: Sein Vater ist Manager in einer Baumwollfabrik. Und seine Mutter hat eine Teilzeitarbeit in einem Call-Center, das einer großen britischen Bank gehört.

Father: Interessant. Hier hatten wir früher auch Baumwollfabriken, aber die meisten mussten wegen der Billigkonkurrenz aus Asien zumachen. Und die englischen Arbeiter sind bestimmt auch nicht über die indischen Call-Center glücklich. Was meint er dazu?

You: My dad says we used to have cotton mills here, too, but most of them had to close due to cheap competition from Asia. And he doesn't think British workers are very happy about

Chapter 3 | Exercises 5–6

Indian call centres. He wants to know what you think about that.

Tariq: OK, it's not an easy subject, but the people in my father's factory have to work. Most of them are very poor, compared to Europeans. And he shouldn't forget that in the early 20th century it was British cotton mills which destroyed the Indian textile industry.

You: Er findet, dass es kein leichtes Thema ist. Verglichen mit den Europäern sind die meisten indischen Arbeiter sehr arm. Sie müssen arbeiten. Er meint auch, dass man nicht vergessen sollte, dass es die englischen Baumwollfabriken waren, die die indische Textilindustrie kaputtmachten.

Father: Gut, aber seine Mutter muss doch nicht arbeiten, oder? Als Manager verdient man auch in Indien ganz gut.

You: Dad wants to know if your mum has to go out to work. He assumes that executives have pretty good salaries in India, too, don't they?

Tariq: Yes, he's right. She doesn't have to go out to work. But we're saving up for a new house, and Mum wants to help out. She's independent and likes to get out of the house.

You: Nein, da hast du Recht. Sie muss nicht arbeiten gehen. Aber die wollen in ein neues Haus umziehen, und sie will mit der Finanzierung helfen. Sie ist recht selbständig und geht gerne aus dem Haus arbeiten.

Tariq: Mum and Dad aren't the only ones involved in globalization. My older sister Sarita is the best in her class at maths and she gives private tuition in maths on the internet to students in Britain and Belgium.

You: Tariq sagt, dass seine Eltern nicht die Einzigen sind, die an der Globalisierung beteiligt sind. Seine ältere Schwester Sarita ist auch dabei. Sie gibt Nachhilfeunterricht im Internet an Schüler in England und Belgien.

Father: Vielleicht könnte sie deiner Schwester helfen. Sie ist schlecht in Mathe, aber gut in Englisch. Frage, was es kostet. Es darf nicht zu viel kosten.

You: Dad says maybe she could help my sister. She's bad at Maths but good at English. How much does your sister charge? It mustn't cost too much.

Tariq: Five euros an hour.

You: Fünf Euro die Stunde.

Father: Fünf Euro die Stunde! Das ist ja spottbillig. Wir zahlen sonst 20!

You: He says we'll do it. We normally pay 20 euros.

Tariq: But I thought you were against globalization …

6 Listening comprehension

starwb-06: audio transcript

Jordan: Gord, what can be done to exert pressure on the Bangladeshi government to improve worker conditions?

Gordon: Well, the industry is really important to Bangladesh. It's worth about $20bn or 10% of its overall economy. Three, four million people have …, depend on it for work, so its exports are really important, and countries like Canada, the United States, the European Union, certainly have some leverage on the Bangladeshi government to get them to toughen up safety requirements, because we let a lot of Bangladeshi goods come in here duty-free or quota-free under preferential access, so if governments, including the European Union, which takes about 60% of the products, start closing those doors, as they may threaten to do, that would hurt the economy and, you know, would cause the government to think twice.

Jordan: And have you seen any indications that the Canadian government will do what it can to help?

Gordon: We haven't heard too much from the Canadian government, but we're relatively small players. Canada takes about 5%, 4% or 5% of Bangladesh's exports. The people who are leading this charge at the moment are the European Union.

Jordan: Joe Fresh, a fashion line sold in Loblaw Stores, was one of the labels being manufactured in the building, and they've promised to provide some compensation to family members, to send auditors to establish new corporate standards. Andrew, have they done enough?

Andrew: I think that's maybe all they can do as one company. I think the focus on Joe Fresh is kind of unfair in the sense that, you know, it's the Canadian angle, right? People know it and it's a kind of marquee retail brand, so in order to bring it home every story in Canada mentions Joe Fresh, but it's not like one company, or even one country, can fix the situation. It's a much bigger issue, and it goes back to … , sort of, pressuring the Bangladesh government, which is really, you know, has a huge interest in keeping this going to first of all enforce its own standards, and to work with other governments and other organizations … other international organizations to raise the standards, which can be done. You know, sometimes it's posed as a kind of all-or-none situation, you know, either we're going to have cheap clothes with poorly paid workers, or we're going to have to pay through the nose for clothes and so forth, and there's lots of things in the middle that can be done, and are being done in other countries which have similar low-wage industries to actually improve things without wrecking their economy.

Jordan: In fact, Sheikh Hasina, the prime minister of Bangladesh, has demanded meetings with retail organizations to do just that. The wages there are absolutely pathetic, a matter of, you know, pennies per hour, $38 a month, but they have actually been increasing, and work conditions, although, again, appalling by our standards, have been increasing, or improving, I should say, a little bit, so the Bangladeshi government does have some leverage.

Source: Toronto Star, editorial podcast, 2.5.2013, http://thestar.blogs.com/files/ed-podcastmay1.mp3

1 a
2 Canada: 4%–5%
   EU: 60%
3 c, d
4 c
5 a
6 b

7 Did you get that?
1 were told
2 arrived at
3 met
4 understand
5 been given
6 receiving
7 become
8 'd/had had to
9 catch

8 Nations and nationalities
1 Finnish/Finns
2 Scottish/a Scot
3 Korean
4 Irish people – Irish people/the Irish
5 Chinese – Chinese (people)
6 Dutch people
7 British people
8 Poles/Polish

9 A slang quiz
1 c   4 b   7 b
2 a   5 c   8 a
3 c   6 a

10 Informal to formal
(Various answers are possible here, for example:)
Dear Sir/Madam
I spent two nights recently from 25th to 27th April with my girlfriend at the Blue Star Hotel in Chalfont Road, Hastings. It was not a pleasant experience. The hotel was poor quality with old furniture, and its facilities were not in (a) good condition. For example, we couldn't adjust the water temperature in the shower. The mattress on the bed was so old that neither of us could sleep. The breakfast on both days was cold, and the fried tomatoes and mushrooms were not fresh. They were out of a tin. This is not the standard I would expect from a hotel which/that charges £100 per night.
When I politely complained to the receptionist, she was not helpful and became annoyed. What is more, when I was eventually able to speak to the manager the next day, he lost his temper and started shouting and screaming abuse at me. The whole weekend was ruined for my girlfriend and myself. I think the best solution would be that you refund the cost of this terrible weekend in full.
Yours faithfully

Chapter 3 | Exercises 11–16

11 Working at a factory

a *(Various answers are possible here, for example:)*
clothes: smocks, underwear, backpacks, duffel-bags, make-up
work: to assemble, payday, paycheck, shift, lose your job
people: security guards, bosses, drivers, cleaners, cooks, janitors, supervisors
facilities: machines, kitchens, dorm(itorie)s, infirmary, customs checkpoint, fire-alarm, barbed wire, padlocked gate

b *(Various answers are possible here, for example:)*
Had to close Miracle Spirit today. We did the usual. To avoid trouble we pulled the *fire-alarm* when the workers changed *shifts*. Once we'd got them out of the building we ran outside and *padlocked the gate*. You could see the women in their *factory-issue smocks* carrying *backpacks*. Some of them had rushed out so quickly that their *underwear* and even their *make-up* had fallen on the ground. I hate doing this, but I have to follow the orders of Head Office. The company cheats them of their last *paycheck*, because we always do it a couple of days before *payday*.

12 Which past?

1. started
2. (had) already had
3. had worked
4. was
5. (had) applied
6. (had) talked
7. ran
8. (had) said
9. was / had been
10. (had) disagreed
11. was
12. exploited
13. remembered
14. had told
15. were suddenly locked

13 Word quiz

a *(Various answers are possible here, for example:)*
garbage: waste food or paper that you throw away; something stupid
junk: things that people regard as useless or of little value
craft: a boat or ship; an aircraft or spacecraft
vessel: a large ship or boat

b A boat is usually smaller.

c 1 a
2 c

d
1 a *AE*   b wrong   c *BE*
2 a *AE*   b wrong   c *BE*
3 a wrong   b *BE*   c *AE*
4 a *BE*   b wrong   c *AE*

14 An interview with Roz

(Various answers are possible here, for example:)
Roz: Well, I was amazed. I hadn't seen a soul for hundreds of miles. Then suddenly I saw this boat. It was really weird.
Interviewer: Can you describe it to us?
Roz: Yes, of course. It was made of thousands of plastic bottles, with a plane's cockpit and a mast.
Interviewer: What were they doing out in the Pacific on a junk raft?
Roz: They were trying to make people aware of the way (that) human beings are polluting the oceans. It's a fantastic idea.

15 More about global warming

1 b
(Various answers are possible here, for example:)
2 Some scientists even think that there is the possibility of a 'runaway greenhouse effect'.
3 The Gulf Stream currently guarantees Europe a milder climate. Any change in the flow of the Gulf Stream would/will lead to Arctic conditions in Europe.
4 This could have enormous economic and social consequences.

16 Where's the apostrophe?

1 The amount of CFCs peaked at the earth's surface 10 years ago.
2 The United States' lead was followed by the majority of countries.
3 If CFC use had continued, today's hole would be much larger.
4 People talked about it over the neighbour's/neighbours' fence.
5 The Montreal Protocol's success was a pleasant surprise.
6 People's attitudes have changed.
7 The United Nations' support has been invaluable.
8 Sara Lajeunesse's article outlines the development.
9 The boss's car stopped at the gate.

Chapter 3 – Living in the Global Village

Focus on Literature: Poetry

1 'Pictures made out of words'

(Various answers are possible here, for example:)

1 c	3 a	5 a	7 d	9 c	11 c	13 d	15 f
2 e	4 c, a	6 b	8 b	10 e	12 a	14 f	16 a

2 Who is the speaker of the poem?

a *(Various answers are possible here, for example:)*

My Life in the Garden by Roger McGough

It is a lovely morning, what with the sun, etc. And I won't hear a word said against it.	poet? Talking to someone who tends to complain about the weather?
Standing in the garden I have no idea of the time Even though I am wearing the sundial hat you gave me.	A female speaker who wears this sort of hat?
What the scene requires is an aural dimension And, chuffed to high heaven, birds provide it.	poet – but obviously the companion is not speaking?
I think about my life in the garden About what has gone before	
And about what is yet to come. And were my feet not set in concrete,	aha, a garden statue with a sundial!
I would surely jump for joy.	

b *(Various answers are possible here, for example:)*
The speaker is a garden statue with a sundial on its head. This becomes clear once you have read that its feet are "set in concrete". The person addressed must be the owner of the garden.

c cf. the highlighted phrases in **1a**
(Various answers are possible here, for example:)
At first I was puzzled, but when I understood that the speaker must be a statue I was amused. I was also surprised, because statues don't think – but the poet is obviously talking about the statue.

3 Sound devices

a

Hinx, minx, the old witch winks, The fat begins to fry	rhymes **plus assonance**
Nobody at home but jumping Joan, Father, mother and I.	assonance

Stick, stock, stone dead,
  Blind man can't see;
Every knave will have a slave,
  You or I must be HE.
	alliteration

b *(Various answers are possible here, for example:)*
It is a poem that is meant to be spoken with emphasis, and all the sound devices give such emphasis. Besides, it is easier to memorize a poem when the words are linked together by rhyme, assonance and alliteration.

c *(Various answers are possible here, for example:)*
In poems not meant for repetitive playful use sound devices are not quite as evident as here. However, certain rhymes and similar devices always serve to emphasize ideas or statements, even when that happens in a more subtle way.

4 Going Places

1 What does it mean?
1c, 2a, 3c, 4b, 5a, 6b, 7c, 8b

2 Alternatives
1. Each year the number of international students increases by 12%.
2. 63% of those surveyed have dated someone who speaks a different language.
3. Over ⅓ of businesses want people specifically for their language skills.

Key to 'Words in Context' wordlist on pp. 46–47

3 Collocations in context
1. e: to gain experience
2. h: broadens your horizons
3. g: meet a new challenge
4. f: a vital opportunity
5. a: contribute to mutual understanding
6. d: boost his self-confidence
7. b: advance my English
8. c: intercultural skills

4 Changing word classes
1. exchange, verb
2. challenged, verb
3. advance, noun
4. essentials, noun
5. volunteers, noun
6. host, verb
7. range, verb

5 Jumbled words
1. host
2. vital
3. boost
4. broaden my horizons
5. accommodate
6. foreign
7. awareness
8. self-confidence

6 Peter's errors
1. Hi, I am a German exchange student who has been in the USA since August 2004.
2. I'm staying with a host family who took the responsibility of looking after me for a year.
3. During the week I go to high school, where I have a lot of interesting classes.
4. I'm trying to get to the point where you guys can't hear my accent anymore.
5. I have already learned many other things since I got here.
6. It's about the best thing that could have ever happened to me.
7. I learned about customs, morals, beliefs, the slightly different food, and lots of other things.
8. I now understand radio and TV shows in the other language.
9. I make friends and contribute toward tightening our cultural bonds.
10. I discovered all the little differences, like in street signs, and my views and everything I took for granted are suddenly just upside down.
11. I've become really open-minded.

7 At a US high school

starwb-08: audio transcript

Sofiya: It was so amazing. You just met people from everywhere.

Zarrina: I learned a lot about the world this year. My name is Zarrina. I'm 18, and I'm from Tajikistan.

Sofiya: My name is Sofiya. I'm from Ukraine and 17 years old. I would suggest you don't expect what you saw in the movies, or whatever, because it's only movies. It's not that ... how life really is. The US is an amazing country. Yes, you can ... just like ... you live in the US, but it's like... you are in every country in the world. Especially at school. Just everybody has an interesting background.

Zarrina: There is this stereotype that Americans are not good in ... In Tajikistan we do a lot of math, a lot of homework and we do a lot of problems at school. But here, it's just a lot less.

Sofiya: And back home you do memorization. You do writing, and like ... you do stuff, and sometimes teachers give you homework that is just impossible to finish. But I don't do that as much as I do at home. You study, you still study. It's just not so stressed.

Zarrina: Here, I think, teachers teach a lot better. At least some of them. And critical thinking is much better here. In Tajikistan it's more memorizing stuff, but not analysing and sharing your thoughts and your ideas about stuff.

Sofiya: And teachers are more kind, really kind compared to home. They respect that you're a person and that you want to learn. Back home, they just scream at you.
I was not expecting, but I thought that because of the movies, I thought that American people are pretty dumb. You know, American people, most of them are pretty dumb. Not dumb, but they don't study as much. It's totally wrong. There are so many smart kids. So many really know what they're talking about. Like they are concerned about government, and they are concerned about ... they read newspapers. I never read newspapers. And here people just ... they want to know what's going on in the country, want to be part of their society. Here, children and parents are not uptight, like back at home. Like, in my family, they're always together. It feels like they live temporarily together.

Zarrina: I notice, at school, that a lot of people just can't wait until they're 18.

Sofiya: They're waiting to go to college and to leave friends, and to leave home, and live their own life. I was homesick only when I just came, and I felt so different, I don't know, my host family ... I [was] just so lost, I want my mom to hug me. But then, after a week or two weeks, I let it go.

Zarrina: ... I just missed everything, but I think I remember the things people were telling me about getting busy.

Zarrina: And you can buy everything, whenever. In Tajikistan we just eat food that's in season, but here you have all these grocery stores that have everything.

Sofiya: I think the problem is there are a lot of sweets, and it's really tempting to eat them all the time.

Zarrina: I like peanut butter.

Sofiya: I think ice cream in the US is the best. So sweet. It's just so delicious.

Zarrina: I think ice cream here has more fat.

Sofiya: Portions are really huge here. It's something like five times bigger. I feel sometimes like I can order one dish and five people can eat and everybody will be full.

Zarrina: I think I started thinking in English. I think knowing English makes me more confident, because ... to be able to talk to more people. A lot of people know Russian, but English is not well taught in schools.

Source: http://blogs.worldlearning.org/now/2013/08/07/flex-podcast-two-exchange-students-from-eurasia-reflect-on-their-year-in-the-united-states

a 1a, 2bd

b 1b, 2b, 3aef, 4b, 5c, 6a, 7ad
8 a: Zarrina likes peanut butter.
8 b: Sofiya likes ice cream.
9 She's started thinking in English.

8 I wouldn't have missed it for the world!
I've been staying in Melbourne now for three months. My host family consists of a host brother, who is my official exchange partner, a host sister and of course two host parents. I'm really enjoying my stay here in Oz, and I'm so glad I chose it for my exchange trip. I came here to revise my English language skills, which seems to have worked, because I'm now much more fluent in the language than I was in the school classroom back home. I tend to pick up a lot of colloquial phrases from my schoolmates, but I also learn useful words by reading the paper and watching TV. By now I think I've got over my culture shock, and I'm beginning to feel at home in Australian culture. To be honest, before I came here I was unaware of how German I really am. You only notice that when you come across people from another culture who were raised with different ideas from those you grew up with. I now feel a lot more open-minded than when I first arrived here. It's been a real privilege to experience everyday life down under. I wouldn't have missed it for the world!

9 Thinking about everyday life in Germany

(Various answers are possible here, for example:)
At school she was struck by the fact that everything was so clean and nobody wore school uniform. We find that perfectly normal, and we don't realize perhaps that in other countries schools look different or that many pupils/ students have to wear school uniform.
Outside school she noticed / she found it striking that the houses were huge and people didn't seem to watch much TV. This made me more aware that other people have different lifestyles and that their everyday life can be very different.

10 Writing an informal email

(Various answers are possible here, for example:)
Hi Roisin
Great to hear from you. That really is fantastic news. I don't think you should worry about the cost. You'll be staying with a family, so they'll pay for most things. All you'll need is a bit of pocket money. You're right – two weeks isn't very long, but I've heard from students who've been on exchanges that you can learn a lot even in two weeks. And it's fun. I went on an exchange to England last year and it was awesome. Much better than learning English at school. So go for it and don't worry.
All the best
…

11 Film techniques quiz

1. high-angle shot
2. eye-level shot
3. long shot
4. close-up
5. zoom
6. low-angle shot

12 What's in it for me?

1. workout: line 31
   brain power: line 28
   (Various answers are possible here, for example:)
   The text says that learning languages helps to increase the power of your brain. It's like a workout in a gym where you strengthen your muscles, but in this case it's the muscles of your mind, your cognitive muscles, not your body's muscles.

2. (Various answers are possible here, for example:)
   It says in the text that in a world which is becoming more and more globalized companies are looking for applicants with multilingual skills because they think these candidates will be more flexible and more capable of understanding complicated problems. By learning a different language you also learn to use new systems of thinking.

3. (Various answers are possible here, for example:)
   The word 'jubilant' means feeling or showing that you are very happy because you have been successful. By choosing to make it jubilant the organizers wanted to prevent or avoid the fear and discomfort which people often feel when they learn or use a foreign language.

13 A hard language?

a
1. vocabulary: I'm doing/taking/sitting (BE) my exams next week.
2. spelling: I don't like to work too much.
3. preposition: Our holiday cottage is on the coast.
4. grammar: I speak English fairly well.
5. grammar: I saw him in town yesterday.
6. preposition: This attitude is typical of him.
7. vocabulary, grammar: I told him that I couldn't come.
8. spelling: I can't find her address.

b (Various answers are possible here, for example:)
It's quite amusing, because it takes irregular forms and uses them to form nonsense words. However, I also think it's misleading, because there are irregular forms in any language and the poem makes it look as if English is more irregular than other languages.

14 Describing and generalizing

(Various answers are possible here, for example:)
In the first photo we can see two teenagers canoeing. They could be on a lake or at the seaside. The large photo in the middle shows a boy and a girl jumping into a lake. In the photo at the top right we can see lots of boys and girls sitting around a camp fire. It looks as if they are toasting something and singing songs. In the fourth photo, a group of young people is playing (beach) volleyball (on the beach).

At summer camps people normally do a lot of outdoor activities, such as swimming, canoeing or playing volleyball. In other words, the people take part in a lot of activities, and there are usually older children or young adults there to give them assistance / to help them in whatever it is they want to do. Some summer camps offer special activities, depending on their location. These might involve sailing, climbing/mountaineering or horse-riding. One of the attractions of camp life is that you can usually choose the activities you want to do yourself.

15 Summer camp in Germany

(Various answers are possible here, for example:)
Dear Chris
You wrote that you were looking for a summer school for water sports in Germany.
Well, I think I may have found something for you. It's called Feriencamp Wellenreiter and is situated near Kiel in Schleswig-Holstein on the Baltic. It's for 15- to 17-year-olds and they offer courses in windsurfing and sailing (from beginners upwards), plus lots of other things like beach volleyball, angling, banana boat riding, wakeboarding, paddling kayaks and canoes.
It costs €650 per week (plus an exam fee if you take an exam), but you can also stay for 2 weeks (€1100) or 3 weeks (€1500). The website says all their instructors speak English, so you should be OK.
There are 3–6 beds (bunk beds) to a room. Each room has its own shower/toilet.
Food and drink are all included. There are three meals a day: a big breakfast, a light lunch and dinner in the evening, which sometimes includes a barbecue. You can have non-alcoholic drinks at mealtimes and throughout the day.
Go on their website and have a look for yourself. It's: www.wellenreiter-feriencamp.de
Yours
…

Focus on Literature: Drama | Exercises 1–3

Focus on Literature: Drama

1 Reading a script

a *(Various answers are possible here, for example:)*
Hear: car crashing against wood, cf. l. 1 ; dialogue mother and son
See: lights come up on living room after the crash noises; elderly lady either standing (walking around?) or sitting on a sofa; her 40-year-old son sitting/standing in front of her

b *(Various answers are possible here, for example:)*
1 up front
2 perhaps sitting at the beginning, and Boolie gets up and paces the room when his mother doesn't give in
3 probably not close enough to touch each other – they keep their distance
4 sofa, easy chair – probably both with flower-print upholstery; part of a table with a flower vase on it …

c *(Various answers are possible here, for example:)*

Line 4
  Boolie: Mama! [starts getting up from his seat]
Line 5
  Daisy: I said no, Boolie, and that's the end of it. [Boolie sits back down]
Lines 6–7
  Boolie: It's a miracle you're not laying in Emory Hospital – or decked out at the funeral home. Look at you! You didn't even break your glasses. [points a finger at her face]
Line 11
  Daisy: I did not! [very loudly, stamping her foot/hitting the armrest with her fist]
Line 12
  Boolie: You put it in reverse instead of drive. The police report shows that. [pointing to table]
Line 18
  Daisy: Think what you want. I know the truth. [looking straight ahead, not at Boolie]
Line 20
  Daisy: No. [hitting the sofa again]
Line 25
  Boolie: Lord Almighty! Don't you see what I'm saying? [Getting up and pacing the room]
Lines 31–34
  Boolie: O.K. Yes. Yes I am. I'm making it all up. Every insurance company in America is lined up in the driveway waving their fountain pens and falling all over themselves to get you to sign on. Everybody wants Daisy Werthan, the only woman in the history of driving to demolish a three week old Packard, a two car garage and a free standing tool shed in one fell swoop! [gesturing to match his words]

2 Looking at the content

(Various answers are possible here, for example:)

a **Daisy:** stubborn (she is not prepared to give in, no arguments can change her mind) – naïve (it was the car's fault) – dignified (she does not get excited, scream abuse, etc.; cf. her description at beginning)
Boolie: polite (stays reasonable, gives arguments, does not abuse his mother) – ironic (cf. his last lines in extract) – frustrated (can't get his mother to see reason)
(Other adjectives also possible, esp. determined.)

b 2, 5

c Daisy will probably play down the accident and focus on her son's suggestions, which she does not accept; Boolie will show his frustration and determination to help her, possibly still hoping to convince his mother, who he respects.

3 Understanding dramatic conflict

(Various answers are possible here, for example:)

a Mother's desire to be independent contrasted with Boolie's feeling of responsibility for her life

b In *Driving Miss Daisy* the atmosphere is one of upset, anger, and frustration, but it is not necessarily explosive. In *Multiple Choice* the characters try to suppress their feelings (adj: *secretive, awkward, worried*), but there is underlying tension because the mother obviously has different ideas about how their son should be brought up/educated than the father, and you know it's also the law that is against her (cf. last words of extract).

Skills Practice

Listening and viewing skills

S1: Listening for information

1 Resurrection

starwb-09: audio transcript

Tom: Let's start with science. What do you think we should be looking out for in 2014?

Oliver: Obviously the most interesting things are the ones we don't know we're looking out for, but one of the things that's on my radar is resurrection. There are various projects around the world which are looking to bring back extinct species. The two most notable ones, I suppose, are ... there's interest in the Pyrenean ibex – technically probably a subspecies, and a gastric brooding frog in Australia. And these species have both had the misfortune to go extinct, but both had the foresight to get bits of themselves saved in freezers before they did so. And so scientists in Australia and Spain are looking at the possibility, and getting some early results with taking the cells in the freezer, putting them into reproductive cells from closely related species and seeing where they can go. The frog's got a little way. The ibex actually got all the way to a new-born ibex, but it was unfortunately rather gruesomely malformed and didn't last very long. That was some time ago, but I believe they're going to start doing that again next year and they might get somewhere. But this fits into a broader thing that's rather fascinating. You say, well, what about those species which did not have the foresight to have parts of themselves frozen for future use, and there's a very interesting new technology called CRISPR, which is a technology for editing whole genomes, and which would allow ... which makes very very precise alterations in genomes on a large scale and can be used to make many alterations at once. And that would allow you to take a close living relative of an extinct species, a sequence of the DNA from the extinct species, which you might get from a university, from a museum or something, and alter the DNA so that you got something considerably more like the extinct species. And that's kind of a fascinating possibility.

Source: www.economist.com/multimedia/sciencetechnology Multimedia Library, Babbage, 1.1.2014

a *individual answers*

b 1 b
 2 b, e
 3 a alterations   d genomes
   b DNA   e species
   c extinct   f technology

2 The Rosetta mission

starwb-10: audio transcript

Tom: OK. So, interesting things happening at the genetic level, then. On a rather different scale, there are some interesting things happening out in space this year. What should we be looking out for?

Oliver: One of the nice things about looking up is that you can make predictions, because the stars move in fairly predictable ways, or rather the planets and the minor planets do, and the minor planet that everyone's going to have to learn to pronounce next year, actually a comet, is comet 67P/ Churyumov-Gerasimenko, which is the destination of a European mission called Rosetta, which will arrive there in May, I think. And this is, I think, the first time that a mission has actually rendez-voused with the comet rather than just watch one fly past at high speed or indeed crashed into one at high speed, as an American mission called Deep Impact did some time ago. And so this will both be able to look at the comet in great detail. It will also be able to track the differences that come to the comet as it moves closer to the Sun, though not disastrously close to the Sun, but certainly

Skills Practice | Exercises 3–4

> close to the Sun. And rather fun, it's also going to launch a probe which will, as it were, land on the comet, though 'landing', it will sort of winch its way to the comet, 'down' is a fairly loose term with gravity as weak as you get on a comet, but that will mark a new way of sampling what actually goes on on a cometary surface. And because comets are relics of the very very early solar system, that should teach people quite a lot about how the solar system actually did form. Hence the name 'Rosetta', which is after the Rosetta Stone, which tells us how ancient languages are related to each other.
>
> Source: www.economist.com/multimedia/sciencetechnology Multimedia Library, Babbage, 1.1.2014

a 1c, 2b

b 1 It will not watch the comet fly past at high speed or crash into it. It will also launch a probe which will land on the comet.
2 It will tell scientists more about the early solar system.

Reading and text skills

S5: Identifying text types

3 Expository, descriptive, argumentative, persuasive or instructive?

A: Text type – persuasive
Reason(s): uses positive words like relief, informed, thoughtful and negative ones such as timid, platitudes, stifle, hand-wringing liberals, airy-fairy and lah-di-dah to influence the reader

B: Text type – descriptive
Reason(s): describes people and events, contains the writer's impressions

C: Text type – argumentative
Reason(s): discusses controversial ideas, the pros and cons, shows a clear line of argument

D: Text type – expository
Reason(s): comprehensive, detailed information, no personal opinion expressed

S6: Reading and analysing non-fiction text

4 'The Summer of the Shark'

a Text type: argumentative
(Reason(s): clear line of argument, discussion of controversial or unusual ideas)

b (Various answers are possible here, for example:)
The excerpt takes the view that the popular image of sharks as a dangerous threat to humans is inaccurate; compared with elephants they are a minor hazard.

c (Various answers are possible here, for example:)
The text uses dramatic, colourful language, e.g. 'chilling', 'rampant', 'carnage' (line 2), similarly 'ripped', 'gorged' (line 4). By including the sensationalist excerpt from *Time* magazine, this effect is increased. Rhetorical questions like 'Scared yet?' (line 10) and 'So why aren't we petrified of them?' (line 23) make the text more lively and therefore interesting. By also asking the question 'But how many shark attacks do you think actually happened that year?' (lines 11–12), which also addresses the reader directly, the authors force the reader to think about how much they really know about shark attacks. This is underlined by the use of the word 'actually', which emphasizes the contrast between what people think they know and what they know. After using statistics to prove that sharks are not a major threat to humans, they underpin this by claiming that a more realistic headline ought to be 'Shark Attacks About Average This Year' (lines 18–19). The figures are then put into perspective by comparing them with the total world population. Finally, deaths due to sharks are contrasted with those caused by 'friendly, entertaining elephants' (line 25), who are a bigger risk to humans. In the final sentence of this passage the authors make a joke about the discrepancy between the image of elephants and the portrayal of sharks as 'villains' (line 26), suggesting that sharks should really have prevented the showing of *Jaws* by taking the film company to court.

d *(Various answers are possible here, for example:)*
I think the authors want to evoke feelings of curiosity in the reader. This is shown by the way they first set the scene, quoting examples of frightening shark attacks, then starting to ask questions which raise doubts about this image, followed by statistics which disprove it.

S7: Reading and analysing narrative prose

5 Gathering information and anticipating plot

a Shane is going to Mendocino by plane – is nervous and takes drugs to calm himself – calls his mother Susan – suspects her partner of dealing in marijuana

b Grandparents sorry to see him go (sentimental?) – mother (Susan) seems to have started a new life in Northern California – Roy Bentley is not a handsome man, so he must have other qualities that attract Susan

c *(Various answers are possible here, for example:)*
Shane is probably expected to change his ways up north, but there may be problems with Roy Bentley (Is he really a marijuana farmer?), and the title suggests that it won't be easy to be good (and stay away from drugs).

6 Identifying the narrator and the point of view

a The narrator is a limited third-person narrator, telling the story from Shane's point of view.

b *(Various answers are possible here, for example:)*
A neutral observer would not see or hear the effects of the drugs on Shane's perception of the interior of the airport. By letting us see and hear what Shane sees and hears the narrator lets us get close to the protagonist and empathize with him.

7 Examining plot development

a – afternoon driving practice
– getting a snack in the kitchen
– emergency phone call from Darren
– driving (with his licence) to pick up Darren in Elk
– Darren's drinking and careless disposal of an empty can
– Darren's confession that he is in possession of drugs
– taking the drugs to avoid detection

b *(Various answers are possible here, for example:)*
– being stopped by the policeman
– being arrested for intoxication and driving without a licence
– court sentence

c *(Various answers are possible here, for example:)*
At first everything seems to be going according to plan, but the phone call interrupts the peace/plans. Shane's decision is risky with regard to timing (his driving test is soon) and the law (he still has no licence). Darren's drinking adds to the riskiness of the situation, and his possession of Speed makes it almost impossible for them to get back to the ranch in time. Their swallowing the pills ends the phase of Shane's 'being good' and actually deserving the Chrysler.

d *individual answers*
Comments should consider Shane's risks (cf. above) but also his willingness to help out a friend in need. He could not know what kind of trouble Darren Grady, who he thought was wise and religious, would get him in by confronting him with drink and drugs (again). He probably should have asked Roy Bentley to help – but perhaps he wanted to try out the car on the highway?

8 Analysing the ending of a story

a *Hints:*
l. 3: changed the oil in the Chrysler
l. 3: He filled the trunk with his belongings
ll. 5–7: She asked him again if he didn't want to transfer to a school in Medocino and stay on with them, but he told her that he missed his grandparents and his friends. 'I might come back next summer,' he said
l. 8: 'You'll probably have the baby by then.'
ll. 8–9: Bentley stuck fifty dollars in the pocket of his jeans. 'You ain't such a bad apple, after all,' said Bentley with a smile.
ll. 9–10: Shane drove off quickly,
Developments:
– Shane must have passed his driving test
– Roy Bentley must have given him the Chrysler despite the incident with Darren Grady
– his mother has had some kind of surgery and is expecting a baby
– both his mother and Roy want Shane to stay with them, but they let him decide
– Roy seems satisfied that Shane behaved unexpectedly well after the incident

– Shane says he 'might come back next summer',
i.e. he isn't ruling out another stay there

b *(Various answers are possible here, for example:)*
thunderstorm: upheaval, anger
rattle windowpanes: upset the foundations of sth.
make chickens flap in their coops: upset peaceful order
clear sky: optimism
free of fog: problems left behind
the highway was still slick and wet from the rain: there were still signs of the storm, the danger is not yet past
scent of eucalyptus in the air: a good environment for a new start

c *(Various answers are possible here, for example:)*
The last paragraph of the story 'Hard to be Good' by Bill Barich shows that for the time being, everything has turned out well for Shane, and also for his mother, who seems to be expecting another baby. The most important indications of this on the content level are the fact that Shane will not be flying home this time, but driving his own car; that he accepts the idea of his mother having another child; that he goes back home to his grandparents on the one hand, but but doesn't exclude another visit next summer, meaning that he wants to go back to his old life, but probably not his old ways. He now knows that he has a real connection to his mother and her partner.

The description at the beginning of the paragraph of the 'unseasonal thunderstorm' that caused windowpanes to rattle and chickens to behave nervously reminds us of the upsetting behaviour of Shane (and his friend), which temporarily disrupted the peace on the ranch. However, the fact that the storm leaves behind a clear sky and no trace of fog clearly indicates that at least for the moment all is really well with and for Shane. However, in the last sentence the writer reminds us that there are still potential dangers when he says that 'the highway was still slick and wet from the rain', which can cause problems when driving – and in the context of the whole story, we are reminded that it is still 'hard to be good'.

The scent of eucalyptus in the air could mean that Shane is taking good memories home with him, making the ending predominantly optimistic despite the risks.

S8: Reading, watching and analysing drama

9 Constructing plot from dialogue

a 1 racing and winning, training together, being a refugee, being a superhero, being an Olympic hero
2 that he has fled from another country on Earth
3 he doesn't understand the references to being a superhero and in particular being an Olympic hero
4 he asks his special watch for information

b The extract is about the meeting of kids from two different planets who think they can help each other, although they have no understanding of each other's backgrounds.

c *(Various answers are possible here, for example:)*
Misunderstandings of references lead to personal misunderstandings and disappointments. ZeeBoy's abnormality may be discovered (metal, batteries, watch) so that he is disqualified and might have to go back home to the war on Zola.

10 Misunderstandings

a **Planet:** Kalina is referring to another country, and when ZeeBoy says 'planet' she probably just understands it metaphorically, as if he was saying 'a completely different place from this one'.
Superhero: On Zola ZeeBoy is actually a superhero, and he is surprised that the category exists on Earth as well. He does not understand the connection between comic books and superheroes, because on Zola they are characters that really exist, not comic-book figures.
Battery: ZeeBoy explains that his system runs on a 24-hour battery, but Kalina takes this to be a metaphor which she repeats when she says it must be 'at max' the next day for the race.

b *(Various answers are possible here, for example:)*
'Weird' often means 'different from the norm', 'not acting as expected', and this is how Kalina uses the word. Of course, a character from outer space, i.e. another planet, is actually 'weird' compared to people on Earth. Kalina does not know that ZeeBoy is made of metal and runs on batteries, but the audience do, so they might laugh at her words.

c *(Various answers are possible here, for example:)*
Kalina is a friendly girl eager to help the newcomer, perhaps especially since she has seen him beat everybody else on the racetrack. At the

same time she is frustrated because the fact that he wins has led to her being third again. She is outgoing, wants to talk to her new acquaintance, but she is also puzzled at how little he knows.

11 Stage directions and props

a 'Beat' (l. 3, l. 15) and 'pause' (l. 30) or 'awkward pause' (l. 16) indicate that there is a break in the flow of the dialogue in which the characters stop to think.
'nervously carries on rambling' (l. 12) indicates that Kalina is not comfortable while she speaks, so she 'rambles', i.e. she speaks without thinking. 'Pointing at Marvel' (l. 17) is a straightforward description of a gesture or of movement, as is 'walks to a quiet spot and speaks to his watch' (l. 45).

b (Various answers are possible here, for example:)
l. 8 (Kalina): *Looking up with surprise*
l. 26 (ZeeBoy): *With anxious excitement in his voice*
l. 27 (Kalina) *reassuringly*
l. 28 (ZeeBoy) *worried*
l. 42 (Kalina) *with a puzzled frown*

c (Various answers are possible here, for example:)
– buildings indicating locker rooms, lavatories etc.
– a race track with a finish line and flags
– a patch of lawn where the two kids sit (nearby, Marvel, and possibly other kids, is/are also standing around)
– towels, water bottles

S9: Reading and analysing poetry

12 Painting images with words
(Various answers are possible here, for example:)
The speaker – either the poet himself or a fictional person who often walks (to work?) on a particular track – often passes a broken-down farmhouse and wishes he could repair it and give it new life, i.e. new residents. He compares the house to a lonely person with a broken heart. The mental image is of a derelict house and its various elements.

13 Examining the structure of the poem

a 7 stanzas of 4 lines each;
rhyme scheme: aabb ccdd eeff gghh iijj kkll aamm (i.e. pair rhymes throughout, with the beginning of the last stanza echoing the beginning of the first stanza)

b The lines have different numbers of syllables in all, but a relatively stable number of stressed syllables – 6 or 7. The rhythm is varied because there is not a regular succession of stressed and unstressed syllables.

c (Various answers are possible here, for example:)
b The poem's regular stanza structure and rhyme scheme give it an effect of controlled walking.
c The succession of stressed and unstressed syllables is varied, so that there is a pleasing rhythm of movement.
g The poem sounds thoughtful.

14 Examining the stylistic devices

a physical descriptions / metaphorical / personification

Whenever I walk to Suffern along the Erie track
I go by a poor old farmhouse with its shingles broken and black.
I suppose I've passed it a hundred times, but I always stop for a minute
And look at the house, the tragic house, the house with nobody in it.

I never have seen a haunted house, but I hear there are such things;
That they hold the talk of spirits, their mirth and sorrowings.
I know this house isn't haunted, and I wish it were, I do;
For it wouldn't be so lonely if it had a ghost or two.

This house on the road to Suffern needs a dozen panes of glass,
And somebody ought to weed the walk and take a scythe to the grass.
It needs new paint and shingles, and the vines should be trimmed and tied;
But what it needs the most of all is some people living inside.

If I had a lot of money and all my debts were paid
I'd put a gang of men to work with brush and saw and spade.
I'd buy that place and fix it up the way it used to be
And I'd find some people who wanted a home and give it to them free.

Skills Practice | Exercises 14–15

Now, a new house standing empty, with ⟦staring window⟧ and door,
⟦Looks idle, perhaps, and foolish, like a hat on its block in the store⟧.
But there's ⟦nothing mournful about it⟧; it cannot be ⟦sad and lone⟧
For the lack of something within it that it has never known.

But a house that has done what a house should do, a house that has sheltered life,
That has ⟦put its loving wooden arms around a man and his wife⟧,
A house that has ⟦echoed a baby's laugh and held up his stumbling feet⟧,
Is the saddest sight, when it's left alone, that ever your eyes could meet.

So whenever I go to Suffern along the Erie track
I never go by the empty house without stopping and looking back,
Yet it hurts me to look at the ⟦crumbling roof and the shutters fallen apart⟧,
For I can't help thinking the poor old house is a ⟦house with a broken heart⟧.

From: *Trees and Other Poems*, Joyce Kilmer, New York: George H. Doran Company, 1914

b *(Various answers are possible here, for example:)*
1: The house catches the speaker's eye.
2: A haunted house would be less lonely.
3: The house needs repairs and residents.
4: The speaker would like to have the house repaired and give it to someone in need of a home.
5: A new house that is empty may look foolish, but never sad and lonely like an abandoned old one.
6: A house that is meant to shelter family life looks so sad when it stands empty.
7: The sight of the house hurts the speaker and reminds him of a broken heart.

c *(Various answers are possible here, for example:)*
The constant repetition emphasises the significance of this particular house, or any house at all, especially for the people who live in it. (In stanza 4, the speaker uses the neutral word 'place' first, and then 'home' as the prime function of a house.)

d *(Various answers are possible here, for example:)*
In stanzas 5 and 6, a 'new house standing empty' is contrasted with an old house that 'has done what a house should do': whereas the new house merely looks foolish because it has never been inhabited and so cannot miss anything, the old house standing empty looks sad and lonely because it no longer serves as a home to people.

e *(Various answers are possible here, for example:)*
l. 2 broken and black; ll. 5, 7: haunted house / house isn't haunted; l. 10 weed the walk; l. 17 standing – staring; l. 22 wooden / wife; l. 24 saddest sight; ll. 27/28 hurts – house – heart. The alliteration (and some assonance as well: l. 8 lonely / ghost; l. 27 crumbling / shutters) emphasize(s) the movement / rhythm – and at the end the final metaphor of the broken heart.

15 The overall development and message of the poem

a *(Various answers are possible here, for example:)*
The speaker first introduces the house to us, and tells us he wishes it was at least haunted. Then he realizes what the house needs and that he would like to have it made back into a home. At this stage he reflects again on the utter sadness of the old abandoned house, contrasting it first with a new house that has never been lived in, and then evoking images of the family life the old house used to shelter. Here the thoughts become very emotional, and the conclusion ('so') in the last stanza, in which the speaker stresses that he looks 'back' whenever he passes the house and that he thinks the house has a broken heart lead to the conclusion that it may have been the speaker's own house and family he has been speaking of, and that he himself has been abandoned and now has a broken heart. (This explains his involvement with the house and the fact that he would like to restore it to 'the way it used to be', l. 15)

b d: When somebody has no loved ones left to hold, this person's heart is broken like a deserted, broken house.

c The emotional development of the poem in the final stanzas conveys the idea that actually the house is a symbol of the speaker's personal loneliness.

Speaking skills

S10: Giving a presentation

16 Good advice?

1 Wrong. You should practise your presentation, e.g. with a friend or a mirror.
2 Wrong. you should not read out the text to your audience. Use notes.
3 Correct. You will keep your audience's attention more easily if your presentation is easy to understand.
4 Wrong. Jokes and anecdotes make the talk more lively and interesting.
5 Wrong. Statistics can be useful if you visualise them, e.g. by using pie charts or bar charts.
6 Wrong. You should look up words that are difficult to pronounce in a dictionary.
7 Wrong. You should keep eye contact as much as possible.
8 Correct. A presentation is less easy to follow than a normal conversation, where you can ask questions and contribute your own ideas.
9 Wrong. All they do is to make your audience less motivated to listen.
10 Wrong. You shouldn't overload slides, which will make them less useful.
11 Wrong. You should summarize important points at the end, because this is your last chance to get your message across.
12 Correct. In some situations you need to provide more information than you can give during the presentation, so a handout is useful.

S11: Communicating in everyday situations

17 Making conversation

a —

b *(Various answers are possible here, for example:)*
Max uses a lot of one-word answers, like 'OK', 'Yes', 'No', which force the other person to work hard to keep the conversation going. Secondly he says a lot of negative things about the UK school and the food, which is embarrassing for the teacher. Max doesn't sound very polite.

c *(Various answers are possible here, for example:)*
Teacher: Hello Max. How are you settling in?
Max: Things are OK in general. I'm sure I'll soon get used to school here.
Teacher: School in Germany is probably a lot different from here.
Max: Yes, it is. We only have school from 8 to 1 most days, but we usually have more homework.
Teacher: Are you having any problems with understanding things?
Max: No, not really. It looks like most of the classes are doing things we did last year in Germany, so that makes them easier to follow.
Teacher: Oh, I'm glad to hear that. How are you getting on with your host family?
Max: They're nice, but I'm not used to British food.
Teacher: Is there anything particular you don't like?
Max: Yes, I'm not so keen on white bread, and I don't really like beans on toast, but maybe I'll get used to them later.
Teacher: Yes, I'm sure we eat different things than in Germany. Is there anything that you like?
Max: I've not been here long enough yet, I'm afraid.
Teacher: Oh dear, well, I hope you get used to things soon.
Max: Yes, I'm sure I will.
Teacher: Well, I've got to rush. See you on Monday.
Max: Yes. It was nice talking to you. Thanks.

Skills Practice | Exercises 18–20

S12: Having a discussion

18 I see what you mean, but …

a

Agreeing with somebody	Disagreeing with somebody	Giving your opinion
Exactly	I don't agree with you there.	I feel that …
I completely agree with you.	I'm afraid I can't agree with you.	If you ask me, …
I think you're right – up to a point.	I'm not sure you're right there.	In my opinion …
(You're absolutely right.)	I see what you mean, but …	I think (that) …
	Oh, come on.	Look at it this way …
	(That's not the way I see it, I'm afraid.)	The way I see it, …
		(I take the view that …)

b *(Various answers are possible here, for example:)*
1 I'm afraid I can't agree
2 I think you're right – up to a point
3 Look at it this way
4 Exactly
5 The way I see it
6 Oh, come on
7 I think

Writing skills

S13: The stages of writing

19 Using linking words

a

Functions	Examples
Organizing the text (O)	firstly, secondly
Giving reasons (R)	because, so, therefore
Adding ideas (A)	also, moreover, what's more
Contrasting thoughts (C)	although, even if, however but
Giving examples (E)	e.g., for example, for instance
Explaining results and consequences (RC)	as a result, consequently

b *(Various answers are possible here, for example:)*
Although many people in the West see a group of tropical islands like the Maldives as a paradise, we are fast destroying that paradise. Scientists have been warning us for many years about global warming. The signs are now clear, even for non-scientists.
Firstly, experts say that we should cut emissions, or half the world will become too hot or too dry for humans. Secondly, scientists are now warning that the ice at the poles is melting much faster than expected. As a result/Consequently, a group of islands like the Maldives, which are only 1.5 metres above sea level, is in danger. Therefore/So climate change for the Maldives is no longer an abstract danger, but a real threat to their survival. Moreover/What's more, if the world can't save the Maldives today, it might soon be too late to save low-lying cities such as/, e.g./for example/for instance London, New York or Hong Kong tomorrow. So/Therefore cutting greenhouse gases is important both for faraway islands in the Indian Ocean and for places nearer home.

S14: Creative writing

20 Debbie's diary

a *(Various answers are possible here, for example:)*
Today was awful. I'm only just getting over it. It all began well. OK, there was the usual two hours standing on a crowded bus full of commuters. I was tired – my day starts at 7 p.m., when most people are going home. It's a relief when I get out of the crowded bus. While I'm walking I practise the clip and the clop. My first call was a clop, so I was Debbie, the married woman with three kids

living in LA, worried about 10-year-old Joey's school grades. At first everything was fine. It was the first call of the day. The American at the other end of the line was explaining his problem. I glanced at the response manual. It gives me all the answers. Easy. I was nearly finished when I spotted Pavithra coming towards me. I smiled at her and at the same time said to the caller, 'Can I be of any other assistance?' As soon as I said it, I knew something was wrong. I'd used the wrong accent! I realized what was wrong immediately and repeated it in Debbie's accent, but it was too late. The caller had noticed. He started to get very aggressive. He was shouting and swearing, said he was going to change his bank. I flipped through the manual, but that didn't help. It was a disaster. I couldn't speak, so I just hung up. It was terrible. I hope I don't lose my job.

b *individual answers*

S15: Writing a formal letter or email

21 Writing a formal email

(Various answers are possible here, for example:)

> Dear Ms Davies
> I wish to confirm that we would like to book Gwyndy Cottage for the first two weeks in July. We would be grateful if you could provide us with your bank details so that I can transfer the money for the deposit to your account.
> Could you please also let me know if towels are included in the rent and whether there is parking for two cars. By the way, is it possible to hire bikes locally?
> I will let you know a few days before we are due to come when we expect to be arriving.
> Yours sincerely
> …
> Contact details: …

S16: Writing an application

22 Writing a CV

Marietherese Biel
117 Louee St., Rylestone, NSW 2798, Australia
Telephone ++61 (0)2-63791058 Mobile ++61 (0)177354796
Email m.biel@gmx.de

Profile	A well motivated, flexible graduate whose aim is to obtain a position as an English-German translator.
Education	
2010 – 2014	Cologne University: BA English (major: 2.3), French (minor: 2.7)
April – June 2012	University of Maynooth (Ireland), Erasmus exchange student
2001 – 2010	Friedrich-Ebert-Gymnasium, Cologne (Germany), Abitur (approx. equivalent to A levels) in June 2010 (average mark: 2.3)
Skills	
Language Skills	Fluent English (C1), good French and Polish (B1), basic Italian (A2)
IT Skills	Good knowledge of MS Office, Open Office, MS Windows, Linux
Work Experience	
September 2013 – present	Easytrip Travel Centre, Rylestone, NSW (Australia)
July 2011 – March 2012, July – October 2012	Freelance translating for firms in Cologne area
2007 – 2009	Private tuition in English and French
2006 – 2009	Tennis coach, Rodenkirchen Tennis Club
Hobbies and Interests	Dancing, tennis, travel, reading
References	Available on request

Skills Practice | Exercises 23–24

23 Writing a cover letter
(Various answers are possible here, for example:)

> Ms Penny Ross
> Human Resources
> Lingua Translation Company
> 22 Dobson St.
> Manchester M3 2ZX
> England
> 20 May 2014
> Dear Ms Ross
> I would like to apply for the job advertised on the Jobs4U website for an English-German translator (Ref. No. 236). I am a native speaker of German with extensive experience of English-speaking countries. I am currently working in Australia, but I also spent 3 months in Ireland as an Erasmus student and three months in the USA.
> I feel that I am suitable for the job because I have already spent a total of 11 months translating for various companies in the Cologne area. I mostly translated from English to German, but also worked together with a native speaker of English to do several translations from German to English. I see from your website that a lot of your work involves translations for engineering firms and teaching hospitals. My employers in Cologne were mainly engineering companies, though I did do two translations for Cologne University Teaching Hospital.
> I would be very grateful to have the opportunity to give you more details of my experience at a personal interview. If you need any additional information, please contact me by email. I finish my present job on June 15 and will be travelling back to Germany shortly afterwards. I will be available for interview from 20 June. Thank you for considering me for the position. I am looking forward to hearing from you.
> Yours sincerely
> Marietherese Biel
> Encl. CV

S17: Argumentative writing

24 Globalization: arguments for or against
b *(Various answers are possible here, for example:)*

Arguments for globalization	Arguments against globalization
1 keeps prices low, quality high	1 has led to greater inequality
2 has brought wealth to poor countries, e.g. South-East Asia	2 financial mistakes spread faster, e.g. US banking crisis
3 can help to bring world peace (countries more interconnected, less incentive to go to war)	3 bad for some people, e.g. US factory workers, Mexican farmers, due to greater competition
4 helps protect environment (put pressure on others, e.g. China)	4 leads to cultural differences between countries becoming less, e.g. Starbucks, McDonald's worldwide
5 makes people more aware of problems in other countries, therefore more willing to help poorer countries	5 diseases can now spread more easily

c *(Various answers are possible here, for example:)*
Starbucks in Manhattan and Moscow, cheaper high-quality products, an inter-connected world. All these are aspects of globalization. So obviously globalization is a good thing, right? Wrong. Globalization has made life better for some, but worse for many others.

When you go abroad, e.g. Moscow or Mumbai, it is reassuring to see something familiar like a Starbucks café or a McDonald's, but do we really want watery coffee and boring food wherever we go? If we travel abroad we want to see different cultures, eat different food – borscht in Moscow and a good hot curry in Mumbai – not the same food we know from home.

Secondly, some people argue that because countries are more interconnected, this is a benefit. There is some truth in this, but it is also true that this has led to more dependence on each other. If something goes wrong in one country, e.g. the US financial crisis or Greece's economic crisis, this can easily cause problems for other countries. Before globalization this danger was less great.

Furthermore, supporters of globalization often claim that it has brought prosperity to some countries, e.g. China, which has become much richer than 30 years ago. Although there is no doubt that this is true, these people often forget that globalization has also meant that many factory workers in the West have lost their jobs because they cannot compete with China's low wages. Even in China, there is great inequality of wealth, with millionaires on the one hand and poorly paid labourers on the other.

To sum up, it cannot be denied that globalization has brought benefits. However, it has also created a world with less cultural diversity, made it more vulnerable to economic crisis and taken the jobs of millions of workers in the West. Was it worth all this just to get cheaper clothes from South-East Asia?

S18: Writing a review

25 'Notes From the Midnight Driver'

a *individual answers*

b *(Various answers are possible here, for example:)*

Structure	Review 1	Review 2
Main part: outline of plot, but without the ending	about Alex (16), drunk while driving, so sentenced to volunteer at old people's home. Hates the work: has to visit Sol(omon) Lewis – irritable, stubborn Yiddish man who insults him. They discover that they both like jazz, become good friends	(no details of plot)
Comments on plot, characters, dialogue	compared with other books in this genre realistic fiction), one of the best: characters so funny	sometimes silly, but made reviewer laugh and cry: deep levels of emotion

c *(Various answers are possible here, for example:)*
Although the review in 2 gives more details about how the reviewer reacted to the book, I think I prefer review 1, because it outlines the plot as well as stating how the reviewer reacted to the book.

d *individual answers*

S19: Writing a report

26 The Apollo Theatre

a *(Various answers are possible here, for example:)*
More than 700 people were inside the Apollo Theatre in Shaftesbury Avenue, in London's West End on Thursday when part of the ceiling collapsed. The collapse occurred 45 minutes after the performance of the play, 'The Curious Incident Of The Dog In The Night-Time' began. The audience suddenly began screaming when part of the ceiling collapsed. Eighty people were injured. One possible cause is that excess water during a very heavy downpour led to the collapse. However, Andrew Lloyd Webber, the theatre's previous owner, gave a different explanation. He said that the building had been in a 'shocking' state ten years ago. He had wanted it to be demolished, but English Heritage had opposed this.

Skills Practice | Exercise 27

b
1. Some of the injured were taken to hospital (by the emergency services) on board London buses.
2. Most of them were discharged (by the hospital) shortly afterwards after they had been treated/after being treated for cuts and bruises (by hospital staff).
3. Although performances at the Apollo have been cancelled until 4 January, the London mayor, Boris Johnson, emphasized that the West End was open for business.
4. The rapid response from emergency services was praised as exemplary.
5. The Mayor stressed that Westminster City Council had assured him that all the necessary safety checks had been made and that additional checks were being carried out to ensure the safety of other historic theatres in London.
6. A Scotland Yard spokesman said that the matter was still being investigated.

S20: Writing a summary

27 Summarizing a newspaper report

a *individual answers*

b

Lines	Main points
1–2	chronic lack of textbooks, poor literacy in Ghana, e.g. Suhum primary school
5–7	example: Jessie, reading aloud from a Kindle (Amazon's e-reader)
13	Kindle gives Jessie access to 140 titles
16–17	now easier for parents to help with homework – always has books she needs
18–21	Kindles distributed as part of iRead 2 programme by Worldreader, charity set up by former Amazon executive and book enthusiast David Rusher
22–25	Kindles less fragile, use less power and less connectivity-dependent than tablets, laptops, making libraries more accessible
25–27	Ghana chosen because has strong economic growth, is a stable democracy, but rural areas remain poor
29	e-readers motivating students to read
30–32	e-readers have made classroom more exciting – everyone has their own book
32–33	early results show concrete results: faster reading speeds, faster listening comprehension rates
37–41	Worldreader successful because uses local content on Kindles – relevant to children's lives, e.g. "Malaria", book about a disease common in Ghana, educates children about prevention
42–44	Kindles have changed teaching, also: if children don't know a word, they look it up on the dictionary in the Kindle

c *(Various answers are possible here, for example:)*

Suhum, like many primary schools in Ghana, has had a problem with a severe lack of textbooks and poor student literacy. Jessie, a student at Suhum, shows how this has changed. She is reading aloud from a Kindle, which gives her access to 140 titles. She says it's easier for her parents to help her with homework, because she always has the books she needs.

The Kindles at her school are part of a programme organized by the charity Worldreader, which was founded by former Amazon executive David Risher. Kindles are less fragile and consume less power than tablets or laptops. The charity chose Ghana because rural areas there are still poor in spite of strong economic growth and a stable democracy.

Teachers claim that the e-readers help to motivate the students. Because each student has their own book, teachers can give them homework. The charity has discovered that use of the Kindles raises reading speeds and rates of listening comprehension levels.

The charity points out that using e-readers results in parents becoming more involved in what their children are doing at school. Children also use the dictionary in the Kindle to look up words they don't know.

It explains that the success of Worldreader is partly due to its aim of encouraging the use of local content on the Kindles, e.g. the book Malaria, which deals with experiences many Ghanaians share.

Mediation skills

S21: Mediation of written and oral texts

28 Mediating German to English

(Various answers are possible here, for example:)
Is Britain's mince pie in danger? The London correspondent of ARD, German television's Channel 1, thinks it is. First of all: what is a mince pie? He explains that it's a small round pie filled with fruit and flavoured with brandy or rum. Now this is being threatened by the invasion of the German Christmas cake, the 'Butterstollen'. Just before Christmas 2013 British supermarkets were selling 24% to 50% more 'Stollen' than in the previous year. One British journalist commented that 'Stollen' was becoming more popular than the traditional mince pies. German supermarket chains such as Aldi and Lidl are even doing better at making mince pies than their British rivals. The consumer magazine *Which?* named their mince pies as being better than the local equivalents. 'Stollen' is not the only import from Germany. Birmingham has had a German Christmas market now for 13 years. It started when Birmingham's twin city, Frankfurt, sent over 24 Christmas market stalls. By 2013 this had grown to 200 stalls, with coaches from all over the country bringing four million visitors in 2012. There are now not many towns or cities in the UK that do not have their own Christmas market. London has several, with stalls selling mulled wine ('Glühwein'), roasted almonds and of course German sausages.
German influence on British Christmas customs has a long tradition. Queen Victoria's German husband, Prince Albert, put up the first Christmas tree in 1848 in Windsor Castle. Others later copied the Royals, and now a Christmas tree is part of British Xmas customs too.

29 Mediating English to German

(Various answers are possible here, for example:)
Im 20. Jahrhundert haben drei große Entwicklungen bedeutenden Einfluss auf sowohl die englische als auch andere Sprachen. Es waren:
1. Zwei Weltkriege, in denen zwei wichtige Siegermächte englischsprachig waren. Besonders im 2. Weltkrieg kamen plötzlich Millionen von Menschen mit Englisch in Kontakt. Nach Kriegsende bestand dieser Kontakt weiter, z.B. durch den Wiederaufbau, den Handel und den Bildungsaustausch.
2. Der Kalte Krieg zwischen dem kapitalistischen Westen und dem kommunistischen Osten, wobei auf der westlichen Seite die Vereinigten Staaten die wichtigste Rolle spielte. Nach dem Zusammenbruch der Sowjetunion 1989 wurden sie sogar zur einzigen Supermacht. In den ehemals kommunistischen Staaten Osteuropas, in denen die englische Sprache nach dem Krieg ohnehin als Sprache der Freiheit gegolten hatte, gewann das Englische noch mehr Gewicht. Nach dem Zusammenbruch der UdSSR wurde diese Position auch in Russland verstärkt, als das Land versuchte, den technisch und wirtschaftlich weit überlegenen Westen einzuholen.
3. Bei der Globalisierung waren die USA von zentraler Bedeutung. Im letzten Viertel des Jahrhunderts entwickelte sich die englische Sprache zum kommunikativen Bindeglied des internationalen Kapitalismus sowie der weltumspannenden Medienlandschaft. Hierbei dominierte die amerikanische Variante des Englischen, die nicht nur andere Sprachen, sondern auch andere Spielarten des Englischen, einschließlich das britische Englisch, stark beeinflusste.

Study skills

S22: Making and taking notes

30 Decoding abbreviations

a
1 Queue here
2 See you at four.
3 Why are you late?
4 Keep it short and simple!
5 You don't need to write every letter in a word to be understood.

b *(Various answers are possible here, for example:)*
1 U cd ask yr tchr
2 Y dnt w mt 4 a cffee?
3 Lts h a pty
4 Wht R U gttng 4 Xmas?
5 How mch hmwrk h U gt 2day?

S23: Dealing with unknown words

31 The Lord above will pay

a —

b *(Various answers are possible here, for example:)*

1	**conductor** – the man who in the past collected money from the passengers on a bus **jangle** – the unpleasant noise made by pieces of metal hitting each other, e.g. coins, keys etc.
2	**timid** – shy
3	**splutter** – to speak quickly and with difficulty, making soft spitting sounds, because you are angry or embarrassed **outrage** – extreme anger, like rage and 'Rage'
3–4	**pudgy** – slightly fat **swivel** – turn around **wobble** – move unsteadily **snigger** – laugh in a quiet, unpleasant way, esp. at someone's problems
5–6	**deliberately** – done on purpose ('absichtlich') **was designed to** – was intended to, planned to **confound** – confuse (French 'confondre' means 'to confuse', i.e. 'verwirren')
8	**sulk** – to refuse to speak because you are angry ('schmollen')
9	**disjointed** – not connected clearly or logically
10	**intimacies** – intimate relations; intimate corresponds to German 'intim'
11	**clerk** – a person who keeps the records in an office, in this case a government office

S25: Using a dictionary

32 Monolingual or bilingual?

monolingual: a, b
bilingual: c, d, e

33 Finding out about words

advice
1 The dictionary says that advice is an uncountable noun, i.e. it can't be used in the plural or with the indefinite article.

contrast
2 On the first syllable in the noun and the second in the verb.

3
	BE	AE
contrast (noun)	[ˈkɒntrɑːst]	[ˈkɑːntræst]
to contrast (verb)	[kənˈtrɑːst]	[kənˈtræst]

eligible
4 It means being able to have or do sth. because they have the right qualifications, are the right age etc.
5 In the adjective it's on the first syllable, in the noun on the fourth syllable.
6 eligible: [ˈelɪdʒɪbl]   eligibility: [ˌelɪdʒəˈbɪləti]

get on
7 a to say how well sb. is doing in a particular situation, e.g. He's getting on very well at school.
   b to be successful in your career, e.g. Parents are always anxious for their children to get on.
   c to manage or survive, e.g. We can get on perfectly well without her.
8 on the second word, 'on'

host
9   It's a verb.
10 It can also be a noun.
11 Like *most*. It's [həʊst] in BE, [hoʊst] in AE.

34 *Dein Tee ist im Ofen*: popular howlers
a *(Various answers are possible here, for example:)*
1 a *Dein Abendessen ist im Ofen.*
   b The word *tea* in English not only refers to a drink. It can also mean a meal, either a light meal eaten in the late afternoon or early evening, or an evening meal which other people call *dinner* or *supper*.
2 a Where do I get help?
   b The word *become* is a false friend. It looks like 'bekommen', but means 'werden'.
3 a I don't like her attitude.
   b The word 'Einstellung', like many others, has different meanings. Here the wrong one has been chosen.
4 a He is very proud of his own organizational ability.
   b There are several errors. Firstly the preposition used after *proud* is wrong. Secondly *own* can't be used with an article like in German. Thirdly, 'Vermögen' has different meanings.
5 a I met her in the corridor yesterday.
   b The mistakes are confusion of *floor* with 'Flur', which look similar, and misuse of the tense by translating the German Perfekt literally as an English present perfect when the simple past is needed.

b *(Various answers are possible here, for example:)* These dictionaries often give you useful hints on usage, e.g. if you look up *tea* in the English-German section it also tells you to go to the German-English section to 'Mahlzeit', where a more detailed explanation of the various words for midday and evening meals is given. You can also use a monolingual dictionary like this, of course.

35 Welcoming tourists
1 a 'pass away' means 'to die'
   b In the nearby village you can buy souvenirs.
2 a 'drop in' means 'to visit', but it could also mean 'dropping into the gorge''
   b I was pleased to receive your enquiry about a room. I can offer you a large bedroom with balcony overlooking a romantic ravine. I hope to see you soon.
3 a 'costume' means 'clothing' – what the writer means is 'custom'
   b I recently became the new owner of this hotel and would be pleased to welcome you here.
4 a 'peculiar' means 'strange', and 'gross' means 'unpleasant, disgusting'
   b We can make special arrangements for large parties.

S26: Using a grammar book

36 Understanding mistakes
(CEG = *Cornelsen English Grammar*, English Edition, Berlin, 2001)
1 Error: tense
   Correction: We visited my exchange partner in Canada last year.
   Explanation: With signal phrases like *last year* we use the Past, not the Perfect, because it's a particular point of time in the past. (CEG, §87)
2 Error: definite article
   Correction: I think Canadian society is fascinating.
   Explanation: Abstract nouns are normally used without the definite article. (CEG, §183)
3 Error: tense
   Correction: We've been learning English for six years.
   Explanation: With *since* or *for* when they mean 'seit' we use the Perfect in English, while German uses the Present. We use *since* with a

Skills Practice | Exercises 37–39

point of time, for with a period of time. (CEG, §84)

4 Error: adjective/adverb
Correction: They spoke too slowly.
Explanation: The last word in this sentence tells you more about the verb, so it's an adverb and needs an -ly ending. (CEG §203)

S27: Working with visual material

37 Describing an advert
(Various answers are possible here, for example:)

a On the left of the picture you can see an elderly man in a red coat. He looks sad, and is obviously meant to represent Father Christmas. The text explaining the message is on the right. It gives details of the Greenpeace campaign and how they want to protest about the situation in the Arctic.

b The text to the right reveals Greenpeace's main message: that the polar ice caps are melting. These are the homes of many extraordinary animals, e.g. polar bears. Greenpeace is also campaigning to help save these habitats from pollution by humans drilling for oil there. The use of Father Christmas, whose home is traditionally regarded as the North Pole, is an eye-catching image before Christmas, when this ad was published. Even if people don't believe in Father Christmas, the advert implies that they need to believe in global warming and support Greenpeace to save these animals from extinction.

c The picture of a sad Santa is pretty effective at Xmas, because it reminds people what is happening in the Arctic. By getting people to text Greenpeace to sign the Arctic petition the organization is making it easy for people to protest at a very busy time of the year.

S28: Working with charts and graphs

38 Irish GDP vs GNP
1 line graph
2 the gross national product
3 the gross domestic product
4 steady increase
5 slight decline
6 sharp decrease in both GDP
7 level off
8 pretty constant

S29: Working with cartoons

39 In return for an increase in my allowance, ...
(Various answers are possible here, for example:)

a The cartoon shows a father in the foreground sitting at the computer. Also in the foreground, on the right, his son is offering him his services as technical support.

b The caption to the cartoon contains the son's offer to his father to provide help with solving his computer problems in return for an increase in pocket money. The cartoonist is making fun of the fact that younger people often have a much better understanding of modern media than their parents.

c I think it is effective, because it refers to a common situation where a younger person has more computer expertise than the older one. The caption provides the humour by getting the son to use language which is typical of adults, more exactly the formal language of a professional technical support business.

Exam Practice

Verbs for tasks ('Operatoren')

1 What do these verbs mean?
1d, 2f, 3j, 4b, 5g, 6a, 7h, 8i, 9c, 10e

Reading and writing

2 Fighting deforestation

a 1b, 2a, 3c, 4ad

b (Various answers are possible here, for example:)
1 She is criticizing Proctor & Gamble for buying palm oil from suppliers involved in deforestation.
2 She accuses them of simply insisting that they are in favour of sustainability.
3 She suggests that they should commit (themselves) to No Deforestation projects and stop trusting the RSPO to certify what palm oil is sourced sustainably.

c 1 persuasive
2 (Various answers are possible here, for example:)
Purpose of text: The purpose of the text is to persuade the reader to support the fight against deforestation. I think it's successful in doing this.
Target audience: The target audience is Greenpeace members and people who sympathize with Greenpeace's aims.
Expressing attitude – use of adjectives and intensifiers, or typographical devices: The author uses adjectives to show her opinion, and emphasizes this by repetition, e.g. on ll. 2–3: 'very real and very serious concerns'. She also uses bold type to emphasize important points, e.g. on ll. 7–8 and 34–36.
Argumentation – use of colourful adjectives, emotional images etc.: The use of colourful phrases such as 'wake up call' (l. 13) makes her ideas sound more interesting. This is also underpinned by the emotional image comparing blind trust in the RSPO to buying a used car without checking it first (an everyday image).
Other methods: She contrasts Mars, whose approach she sees as positive, with P&G's, which she regards as negative (ll. 4–6). By addressing her readers directly with 'you' she keeps their attention, e.g. ll. 9 and 10. By using informal language, e.g. 'folks' (l. 13), 'shaky' (l. 18) or 'a lemon' (l. 32) she makes the text more appealing for her potential audience. Finally she hammers home her message by using imperatives to say what her readers should do: 'Tell P&G …', 'Take action here.' (ll. 35–36).

d *individual answers*

3 Rise of the open-source coder generation

a —

b 2 false: cf. ll. 1–2
3 true: cf. ll. 4–5
4 true: cf. ll. 9–11
5 not in text
6 true: cf. l. 21
7 not in text
8 false: cf. ll. 30–32
9 false: cf. ll. 33–35
10 true: cf. ll. 39–41
11 true: cf. ll. 41–43

c 1 expository
2 1k, 2c, 3a, 4d, 5g, 6f, 7b, 8h;
nicht verwendet: e, i, j

Listening

4 Ozone hole history offers climate lesson

starwb-11: audio transcript
This is Scientific American 60-Second Earth. I'm David Biello. Your minute begins now. In the 1970s, chemists Mario Molina and Sherwood Roland found that mundane household items posed a serious worldwide threat. The two chemists discovered that chlorofluorocarbons, or CFCs, from air conditioners and canisters of hair spray could destroy the ozone layer. That insight got them a Nobel Prize. By the 1980s, folks like then Secretary of State George Shultz woke up to the threat, despite a campaign of denial from scientific doubters. He convinced President Reagan that the danger was real and that action was necessary. By

1989, the U.S. and the rest of the world had crafted an international treaty to curb CFCs known as the Montreal Protocol.

As a result, the hole in the ozone layer that forms above Antarctica has mostly stabilized. Now we know that Montreal also bought us a little more time to deal with another air pollution problem: climate change. That's according to a new analysis in the journal Nature Geoscience. The study found a statistically significant correlation between the onset of the Montreal Protocol and a reduction in the pace of global warming. Because CFCs are also greenhouse gases.

The finding is good news. It shows that cutting back on greenhouse gas pollution can slow catastrophic climate change. Sadly, the campaign of denial against global warming continues, denying us the chance to make the necessary response.

Source: http://www.scientificamerican.com/podcast/episode/ozone-hole-history-offers-climate-l-13-11-10/

a b

b 1b, 2bf, 3a, 4a, 5b, 6c, 7c

5 'Bottle boards' ride new wave of recycling

starwb-12: audio transcript

Aspiring surfers along Lima's coast are making waves. Conventional surfboards are built of fibreglass, but these are made of disposable plastic bottles, collected along the beaches near Lima. The boards are inexpensive and eco-friendly. Designer Carlos Pino says the bottles are helping him make the sport of surfing available to kids who couldn't otherwise afford it.

"My childhood was tough, from a young age, and thanks to my father, who was a lifeguard, I learned to swim, and respect the sea, and above all I learned to surf, but for me, being able to practise the sport was impossible."

But for a new generation practising the sport is now possible, with Pino's hand-made surfboards. To make the boards, Pino fills the bottles with dry ice, to keep them firm and then plasters them together with fibreglass to give them form. He says it takes about 51 bottles to make a board. Johnny Leneres is an experienced surfer. He says Pino's boards are ideal for kids who want to learn.

"I think the surfboard is a good idea for kids, very good indeed. It's worth it."

And director of the surfing project, Nadia Balducci, agrees, pointing to the environmental benefits that come with it.

"The idea of this project is to create awareness among young people, and encourage them to take action against the problem of plastic pollution, and doing it through surfing, which connects them to the environment."

That connection, says Pino, is what will ensure that the next generation of surfers connects the beauty of their sport with the beauty of their environment.

Source: http://www.scientificamerican.com/video/bottle-boards-ride-new-wave-of-recycling/

a b, e

b 2 fibreglass
3 (recycled) disposable plastic bottles
4 inexpensive, eco-friendly
5 tough childhood, father lifeguard, couldn't afford surfboard
6 bottles filled with dry ice to keep them firm, then plastered together with fibreglass to give them form (51 bottles per board)
7 director of the surfing project
8 good idea: creates environmental awareness among young

Mediation

6 Kölner Tafel e.V.

a —

b (Various answers are possible here, for example:)
The Cologne charity Kölner Tafel e.V. was set up in June 1995. It was influenced by the US charity City Harvest and similar German organizations. A lot of food in Cologne is thrown away every day because too much is produced or bought or because the colour or weight does not conform to the regulations. At the same time, there are many people in Cologne who do not have enough to eat. The charity uses refrigerated trucks to collect tonnes of donated food from supermarkets, bakeries and manufacturers. Many donate every day, others less regularly. The food is then passed on to places which need it. The charity currently has about 80 helpers. Every year it moves about 750 tonnes of food. Its seven refrigerated lorries travel a distance of 110,000

km each year. The charity is supported by donations of money and goods and by membership fees.

7 Globalized people

You: Er ist zwar Amerikaner, aber einige seiner Vorfahren waren aus England, aber die andere Hälfte der Familie stammte aus Irland, und es gibt sogar ein paar Deutsche in der Familie.

...

You: He says it's something similar with them. Part of his family comes from Greece. Before the First World War there were a lot of Turks in Greece. An uncle of his lives in Cyprus. He speaks English very well. But Ahmet's family come from Izmir. It's on the west coast of Turkey.

...

You: Er fragt, wie lange Sie schon hier sind.

...

You: He says he's been here for over 20 years. He came over to Germany with his wife in 1983. At first he worked / was working in a factory. He saved up lots of money and borrowed the rest of the money from his cousin and bought this shop. He's had this shop now for twelve years.

...

You: Er meint, das ist so ein bisschen wie der amerikanische Traum. Sein Großvater hat auch so angefangen, in den 40er Jahren. Er hat ein kleines Süßwarengeschäft aufgemacht. Später wurde daraus ein Supermarkt. Sein Vater hat dann weitere Supermärkte aufgekauft, und jetzt besitzt die Familie eine Supermarktkette in der Gegend von Chicago.

Speaking (monologue)

8 Environmental protest

a *(Various answers are possible here, for example:)*
  1 background: a forest; foreground: a lot of trees cut down; also in foreground: large Greenpeace banner protesting against rainforest destruction
  2 authentic picture of forest and trees cut down (contrast), plus Greenpeace banner explaining why Greenpeace is protesting
  3 *individual answers*

b *individual answers*

9 Cartoon

a *(Various answers are possible here, for example:)*
  1 foreground: two elderly men sitting in comfortable armchairs talking, both drinking alcohol (wine? cognac?) in fairly luxurious surroundings, possibly a gentlemen's club; background: portraits on walls; conversation confirms: used to luxury
  2 the two men are portrayed positively – comfortable surroundings, relaxing; cartoonist's point made in caption: implies that cliché 'Money can't buy happiness' only part of story – money makes a more luxurious lifestyle possible: this can make people happy
  3 *individual answers*

b *individual answers*

Speaking (dialogue)

10 To gap, or not to gap: that is the question

(Various answers are possible here, for example:)

You: That's not the way I see it, I'm afraid, I think going abroad for a gap year is useful. It definitely broadens your horizon.

...

You: I mean seeing a different country, perhaps improving your English or French or Spanish, getting to know a different culture.

...

You: Another thing is that spending a year abroad looks good on your CV. Employers and universities like kids who've seen a bit of the world before they start a job or start studying. They think they're more mature. I think they're right.

...

You: Sorry, could I just stop you for a moment? You say/said he enjoyed it. That's also important, isn't it? Doing Abitur is pretty stressful, so you need a break between school and a job or before you go to uni, because you have to work hard for both. What's more, you can work while you're abroad, so a stay abroad doesn't have to be expensive.

'Words in Context' wordlists

There are various answers possible, those given in the 'Memory support' column are suggested answers.

Chapter 1 'Teen years, in-between years' SB p.12

Word/Phrase	Memory support	German
a stage of life	Adulthood is a stage of life when a person is usually at their peak level of performance.	ein Lebensabschnitt
a period of transition	Because adolescence is a period of transition from childhood to adulthood, teenagers often feel unsure of themselves.	eine Übergangszeit
(to) assert yourself	WORD FAMILY: assertion – assertive – assertiveness	sich durchsetzen, sich behaupten
(to) play an active role	OTHER COLLOCATIONS: a key/vital/major role	eine aktive Rolle spielen
(to) come of age	In the past adolescents came of age at 21, but nowadays in most countries it's 18.	volljährig/mündig werden
(to) have rights and responsibilities	You need to become aware of the rights and responsibilities you have as an adult.	Rechte und Pflichten haben
(to) gain acceptance	Many young people try to gain acceptance from their own peer group.	Anerkennung finden
a peer group	For many teenagers, the opinion of their peer group is more important than that of their parents.	eine Peergroup (*Gruppe etwa Gleichaltriger*)
peer pressure	For many teenagers, peer pressure is much more important than the influence of their parents or teachers.	Gruppendruck, gegenseitiger Druck
self-confident	Tom always seems so self-confident – he looks very sure of himself, whatever he does.	selbstbewusst
self-conscious	She was very self-conscious when she began her presentation. She didn't look at the audience and fiddled with her hair all the time.	befangen, gehemmt
popularity	She didn't increase her popularity when she started making fun of their friends.	Beliebtheit
(to) be exposed to influences	WORD FAMILY: (to) expose – exposure – exposé – exposition	Einflüssen ausgesetzt sein
under pressure	OTHER COLLOCATIONS: peer pressure / pressure group / high pressure	unter Druck
(to) meet your parents' expectations	Many children find it difficult to meet their parents' expectations.	die Erwartungen seiner Eltern erfüllen
(to) gain admission to a university	OTHER COLLOCATIONS: (to) gain access to sth. – (to) gain time/ground – (to) gain experience/confidence/strength	einen Studienplatz bekommen, an einer Universität (zum Studium) zugelassen werden

'Words in Context' wordlists

Word/Phrase	Memory support	German
(to) give serious consideration to one's future	Once they had finished school, they knew it was time to give serious consideration to their futures.	sich ernsthaft mit seiner Zukunft befassen, ernsthaft über die eigene Zukunft nachdenken
(to) submit to the pressure to conform	WORD FAMILY: conformity – conformist	sich anpassen
(to) strive hard	We are striving hard to become the best in our field.	sich sehr anstrengen, sich sehr bemühen
(to) reach your personal goals	OTHER COLLOCATIONS: (to) reach a level/speed/stage/target – (to) reach a conclusion/decision/compromise	die persönlichen/selbst gesteckten Ziele erreichen
(to) take risks	I think it's better to take risks than never to do anything new or unusual.	Risiken eingehen, etwas riskieren
(to) test your limits	Athletes need to test their limits if they want to improve their performance.	an die eigenen Grenzen gehen, die persönlichen Grenzen (aus)testen
a role model	Teenagers' role models may be other teenagers, rock stars, film stars, even teachers or parents.	ein Vorbild
(to) tend to experiment	Most people tend to experiment with different approaches when they start work.	zum Experimentieren/Ausprobieren neigen
(to) rebel against sth. [rɪˈbel]	WORD FAMILY: rebel [ˈrebl] – rebellion – rebellious – rebelliousness	sich gegen etwas auflehnen
provocative [prəˈvɒkətɪv ☆ prəˈvɒːkətɪv]	That was a very provocative remark you made!	provozierend, anstößig, (sexuell auch) aufreizend
(to) yearn for security	He rebelled against his parents, but he really yearned for security and a stable family life.	sich nach Sicherheit/Geborgenheit sehnen

Chapter 2 'Keeping in touch in the 21st century' SB p. 38

Word/Phrase	Memory support	German
(to) use search engines	We can use search engines to look for information on the world wide web.	Suchmaschinen (be)nutzen
(to) retrieve information	It's much easier to retrieve information from the Internet than from older, traditional sources.	Informationen abrufen
(to) upload content to the net	You can upload your essay to the internet and make it available to other potential users.	Inhalte ins Internet hochladen/stellen
(to) gain access to a global audience	OTHER COLLOCATIONS: global warming/ban/approach/village worldwide/TV audience	sich Zugang zu einem weltweiten Publikum verschaffen
a contributor [kənˈtrɪbjətə]	WORD FAMILY: (to) contribute – contribution – contributory	ein Mitwirkender, ein Beitragender

'Words in Context' wordlists

Word/Phrase	Memory support	German
a hand-held device	OTHER COLLOCATIONS: portable/marketing/labour-saving/water-saving device	ein Handgerät, ein kleiner handlicher Computer
(to) go portable	Information nowadays is going portable, with smartphones and notebooks dominating.	tragbar/transportierbar/mobil werden
information available online	Information about all our products are also available online.	online verfügbare Informationen
(to) access information ['ækses]	WORD FAMILY: access (n.) – accessible – accessibility	auf Informationen zugreifen, Informationen abfragen
a wireless connection	OTHER COLLOCATIONS: wireless network/access/information technology	eine drahtlose Verbindung
(to) enhance the usefulness of sth. [ɪn'hɑːns ☆ ɪn'hæns]	Apps can greatly enhance the usefulness of your smartphone.	die Nützlichkeit von etwas verbessern/erhöhen
(to) influence the way we do sth.	Digital communications technology influences the way we communicate with each other.	Abläufe beeinflüssen
text-based communication	Texting is one of the factors that have led to an increase in the use of text-based communication.	textbasierte Kommunikation
social networking sites (SNS)	Social networking sites have also become areas of criminal activity.	soziale Netzwerke
instant messages	Instant messages have greatly increased the speed of communication between individuals.	Sofortnachrichten, Chatmitteilungen
(to) link people	WORD FAMILY: link (n.) – linkage – link man – link-up	Menschen verbinden
(to) appeal mainly to a young audience	Hiphop appeals mainly to a young audience – most older people prefer quieter music.	hauptsächlich junge Menschen ansprechen
(to) make new contacts	Many people use social networking sites to make new contacts.	neue Kontakte knüpfen
(to) post photos/ messages	OTHER COLLOCATIONS: (to) post a letter/a notice on the notice board/results	Fotos/Nachrichten posten
a false sense of security	The many safeguards of privacy of the individual in the Constitution can easily create a false sense of security in this age of cyberespionage.	ein trügerisches Gefühl der Sicherheit
personal information	I don't want my personal information to be available to foreign countries or big business.	persönliche/private Informationen
the anonymity of cyberspace	The anonymity of cyber-space also encourages Internet trolling.	die Anonymität des Cyberspace
a cyberbully	WORD FAMILY: cybercafé – cybernaut – cyberspace – cyberespionage	ein/e Cybermobber/in, ein/e Internetmobber/in
(to) torment sb.	The cyberbullies tormented Sarah so long that she decided to leave school altogether.	jdn. quälen

Word/Phrase	Memory support	German
a victim	WORD FAMILY: (to) victimize – victimless	ein Opfer
a legal consequence	What would the legal consequences of these internet threats to leading personalities be?	eine rechtliche Konsequenz, eine Rechtsfolge

Chapter 3 'Life in a global village' — SB p. 62

Word/Phrase	Memory support	German
(to) overcome distances	We can easily overcome distances with modern digital communication.	Entfernungen überwinden
modern technology	WORD FAMILY: technologist – technological – technologically	(die) moderne Technik, heutige Technologien
(to) rely on sb.	I'm relying on you to help me with this homework.	sich auf jdn. verlassen
(to) connect virtually with sb. ['vɜːtʃuəli]	Social networks enable us to connect virtually with people all over the world.	mit jdm. virtuell in Kontakt treten/stehen
(to) spread news	News spreads very quickly on social networks these days.	Nachrichten verbreiten
(to) become interconnected	As the world becomes more interconnected, nation states seem to be becoming increasingly out of date.	verbunden/vernetzt werden
(to) become increasingly interdependent	Countries have become increasingly interdependent over the past century.	zunehmend voneinander abhängig werden, immer stärker miteinander verschelzen
a large multinational corporation	Large multinational corporations often have more power than some governments.	ein großes multinationales Unternehmen
(to) outsource the production	We outsource all our production to reduce costs.	die Produktion (an einen externen Dienstleister oder ins Ausland) verlegen
a developing country	WORD FAMILY: (to) develop – development – developer – developmental	ein Entwicklungsland
wages (pl)	The factory workers went on strike for higher wages.	Lohn, Gehalt
western consumers [kən'sjuːməz]	WORD FAMILY: (to) consume – consumable – consumption – consumerism	(die) Verbraucher in den westlichen Industriestaaten
(to) have an impact on sth.	These changes will have an enormous impact on the environment.	starken Einfluss auf etwas haben
deforestation [ˌdiːfɒrəs'teɪʃn]	WORD FAMILY: forest – forestry – forester – forested – (to) deforest – (to) afforest – afforestation	Entwaldung, die Abholzung von Wäldern
water pollution	OTHER COLLOCATIONS: air/noise/light pollution – local/industrial pollution	Wasserverschmutzung

Word/Phrase	Memory support	German
depletion of the ozone layer [dɪˈpliːʃn]	Depletion of the ozone layer could be a serious danger to health.	Abbau/Schädigung der Ozonschicht
global warming	OTHER COLLOCATIONS: the global village/market – global player – global teamwork/solutions	die globale Erwärmung
climate change	WORD FAMILY: climatic – climatology – climatologist – climatological	Klimawandel
environmental damage	OTHER COLLOCATIONS: environmental pollution/impact/problem/influence – environmental issue/movement/group	Umweltschäden
global teamwork	We need global teamwork to solve our environmental problems.	globale Teamarbeit, weltweite Zusammenarbeit
an industrial country	OTHER COLLOCATIONS: industrial estate (BE)/industrial park (AE) – industrial relations/action	ein Industrieland/-staat, ein industrialisiertes Land
(to) live in a sustainable way	WORD FAMILY: (to) sustain – sustainable – sustainability	nachhaltig leben, ein nachhaltiges Leben führen
natural resources [rɪˈsɔːsɪz ☆ ˈriːsɔːsɪz] (pl)	The exploitation of natural resources is increasing rapidly in Brazil and Australia due to greater demand from China.	natürliche Ressourcen, Naturschätze
international cooperation	We need much closer international cooperation if global warming is to be contained.	internationale Kooperation/Zusammenarbeit
a non-governmental organization (NGO)	NGOs are charities or other organizations which are completely independent of governments.	eine Nichtregierungsorganisation, eine nicht staatliche Organisation
(to) agree on rules	One of the biggest problems is how to agree on rules about how to combat climate change worldwide.	sich auf Regeln/Bestimmungen einigen
a common problem	OTHER COLLOCATIONS: a common goal/idea/heritage	ein gemeinsames/allgemeines/häufiges Problem

Chapter 4 'The importance of speaking languages' SB p.88

Word/Phrase	Memory support	German
a foreign language [ˈfɒrɪn]	I love the kick of going to foreign countries, seeing different things and speaking foreign languages.	eine Fremdsprache
essential	Experience is essential for this job.	unabdingbar
a lingua franca [ˈlɪŋgwə ˈfræŋkə]	Because of the many different local languages, Swahili and English are important lingua francas in East Africa.	eine internationale Verkehrssprache (*verschiedener mehrsprachiger Länder*)
a native language	OTHER COLLOCATIONS: a native speaker	eine Mutter-/Heimatsprache

Word/Phrase	Memory support	German
(to) **advance your English** [əd'vɑːns ☆ əd'væns]	OTHER COLLOCATIONS: (to) advance your career/your knowledge/ the cause of democracy	(seine) englischen Sprachkenntnisse verbessern
intercultural skills	In the days of globalization, intercultural skills are just as important as good qualifications.	interkulturelle Fähigkeiten
a school exchange [ɪks'tʃeɪndʒ]	OTHER COLLOCATIONS: school exchange – exchange of insults/ideas – exchange of prisoners	Ein Schüleraustausch
a host country [həʊst ☆ hoʊst]	OTHER COLLOCATIONS: host family/parents/computer	ein Gastland (host = Gastgeber)
(to) **gain experience of a different culture**	OTHER COLLOCATIONS: (to) gain confidence/strength/access/entry	Erfahrungen über eine andere Kultur sammeln/gewinnen
(to) **develop an awareness of different nations**	School exchanges help pupils to develop an awareness of different nations.	ein Bewusstsein für andere nationen entwickeln
(to) **contribute to** sth.	WORD FAMILY: contribution – contributor – contributory	zu etw. beitragen
mutual international understanding ['mjuːtʃuəl]	OTHER COLLOCATIONS: mutual admiration/respect/support – mutual dislike/distrust	gegenseitige internationale Verständigung
a vital opportunity ['vaɪtl]	You shouldn't miss this vital opportunity to study abroad.	eine gute Gelegenheit, eine große Chance
(to) **broaden your horizons**	If you want to broaden your horizons, spending a year abroad is one of the best things you can do.	den eigenen Horizont erweitern
(to) **accommodate** sb.	This hotel can accommodate up to 500 guests.	jdn. unterbringen
abroad	We often go on holiday abroad.	im Ausland, ins Ausland
a range of activities	There's a wide range of activities at the summer camp.	eine Reihe/Vielzahl von Aktivitäten
(to) **be given the opportunity to do** sth.	They were given the opportunity to go on a school exchange to the USA.	die Chance bekommen, etwas zu tun
volunteering	WORD FAMILY: volunteer (n.) – volunteer (v.) – voluntary	ehrenamtliche Arbeit, Freiwilligendienst
(to) **meet new challenges**	She decided it was time to meet new challenges and find herself a new job.	sich neuen Herausforderungen stellen
a life-changing experience	WORD FAMILY: life-enhancing – life-giving – life-saving – life-threatening	eine lebensverändernde/ unvergessliche Erfahrung
(to) **boost** sb.'s **self-confidence**	Coping successfully with difficulties will boost your self-confidence.	jemandes Selbstbewusstsein stärken
(to) **last a lifetime**	If you want friendships to last a lifetime, you have to keep in contact.	ein Leben lang halten/ andauern

Context
Starter

Introduction

Dear student,

Welcome to your **Context Starter** Workbook – Language, Skills and Exam Trainer. The main aim of this *Workbook* is to give you a complete training programme to deal with the vocabulary, structures and skills in **Context Starter**.

In the first part of the *Workbook* (pp. 4–55), you will find a wide range of exercises closely linked to the four chapters of the Student's Book (SB), for example …
- **vocabulary** and **grammar** exercises,
- **Words in Context wordlists** that you can download and edit yourself,
- **listening comprehension** tasks to practise your listening skills,
- extra practice linking up with the **Focus on Skills** and **Focus on Language** sections in the Student's Book,
- pages clearly linked to the four **literature modules** in *Context Starter*.

The second part of the Workbook (pp. 56–103) is made up of …
- **Skills Practice**, with exercises and tips linked to the 'Skills File' in the SB (there are references to this section after many exercises in the WB),
- **Exam Practice**, to help you to lose your fear of tests and exams,
- an **Exercise Finder** with lists of all the WB exercises that practise vocabulary, a point of grammar or a particular skill.

Furthermore, the *Workbook* includes …
- **CHALLENGE** exercises for those who want something more difficult to get their teeth into,
- **vocabulary** and **tip boxes** to support you at difficult points,
- **webcodes** linking you to the audio files and transcripts of the listening tasks, or to the *Words in Context* wordlists.

In addition, the contents of the *Workbook* should be fun too, as we get you to puzzle over why somebody is talking about a 'ketchup strategy' (p. 9), teach you some useful US slang (p. 37), ask you whether you'd like somebody to be your 'tosh' (p. 46) and tell you the real truth about sharks (p. 60).

We hope that by making you feel more at home in English we'll also help you to access the complexity and variety of the English-speaking world.

Your Trainer Team

Symbols used in the WB:

Webcode starwb-01	can be entered at www.cornelsen.de/webcodes to connect you directly to audio files and transcripts (for listening tasks) or to wordlists (for *Words in Context*).
CHALLENGE	marks a more demanding task.
📝	indicates that you should write the answer to this task in your exercise book.
SB A4 ◄	refers to Part A4 of the relevant chapter of the **Context Starter** Student's Book.
► S14: Creative writing, WB pp. 73–74	refers to the *Skills Practice* section of the WB: Skill 14 on pages 73–74.

Abbreviations used in the WB:

adj	adjective	**fml/infml**	formal/informal	**p./pp.**	page/pages
adv	adverb	**i.e.** (*Latin*)	*id est* = that is; in other words	**pl**	plural
AE/BE	American English / British English			**sb./sth.**	somebody/something
cf.	confer, see	**jdm./ jdn.**	jemandem/ jemanden	**sl**	slang
e.g. (*Latin*)	*exempli gratia* = for example	**l./ll.**	line/lines	**v**	verb
etc. (*Latin*)	*et cetera* = and so on	**n**	noun		

Contents

Page			Exercises
	Chapter 1	**The Time of Your Life**	
4	Lead-in		1
5	Words in Context	Teen years, in-between years	2–4
8	Part A	Hopes, fears and realities Focus on Language PRONUNCIATION	5–8
10	Part B	Spread your wings Focus on Skills WRITING	9–15

15	**Focus on Literature (1)** Narrative Prose – the Novel	1–2

Page			Exercises
	Chapter 2	**Communicating in the Digital Age**	
17	Lead-in		1–2
18	Words in Context	Keeping in touch in the 21st century	3–5
21	Part A	Changing ways of communicating Focus on Skills WRITING Focus on Skills LISTENING	6–8
24	Part B	Parents, friends and strangers Focus on Language GRAMMAR	9–16

28	**Focus on Literature (2)** Narrative Prose – the Short Story	1–3

Page			Exercises
	Chapter 3	**Living in the Global Village**	
30	Lead-in		1–2
	Words in Context	Life in a global village	3–4
34	Part A	Global citizens Focus on Skills MEDIATION Focus on Language VOCABULARY AND STYLE	5–12
39	Part B	Looking after the global village Focus on Skills WRITING	13–16

41	**Focus on Literature (3)** Poetry	1–3

Page			Exercises
	Chapter 4	**Going Places**	
43	Lead-in		1–2
44	Words in Context	The importance of speaking languages	3–5
47	Part A	In a foreign classroom Focus on Skills VIEWING Focus on Skills READING	6–13
52	Part B	Work and life experience	14–15

54	**Focus on Literature (4)** Drama	1–3

Contents

Skills Practice

Page			Exercises
	Listening and viewing skills		
56	S1	Listening for information	1–2
	Reading and text skills		
57	S3	Marking up a text	
58	S5	Identifying text types	3
60	S6	Reading and analysing non-fiction	4
61	S7	Reading and analysing narrative prose	5–8
64	S8	Reading, watching and analysing drama	9–11
66	S9	Reading and analysing poetry	12–15
	Speaking skills		
69	S10	Giving a presentation	16
70	S11	Communicating in everyday situations	17
71	S12	Having a discussion	18
	Writing skills		
72	S13	The stages of writing	19
73	S14	Creative writing	20

Page			Exercises
74	S15	Writing a formal letter or email	21
75	S16	Writing an application	22–23
76	S17	Argumentative writing	24
77	S18	Writing a review	25
78	S19	Writing a report	26
79	S20	Writing a summary	27
	Mediation skills		
81	S21	Mediation of written and oral texts	28–29
	Study skills		
84	S22	Making and taking notes	30
84	S23	Dealing with unknown words	31
86	S25	Using a dictionary	32–35
89	S26	Using a grammar book	36
90	S27	Working with visual material	37
91	S28	Working with charts and graphs	38
91	S29	Working with cartoons	39

Exam Practice

Page		Exercises
92	Verbs for Tasks ('Operatoren')	1
92	Reading and writing	2–3
97	Listening	4–5
98	Mediation	6–7
100	Speaking (monologue)	8–9
101	Speaking (dialogue)	10

Exercise Finder

102

104 Acknowledgements

1 The Time of Your Life

Lead-in

1 Describing someone's life SB L-i

a Write a short description of the life of the person you chose in task **1a** of the SB (p. 10). Write your text from that person's point of view. The vocabulary in the box below will help you.

> **In my spare time:** go hiking/backpacking • paint • spend most of/a lot of my time with my boyfriend/girlfriend • do rock-climbing • hang out with friends • play in a band
> **At work:** help as an aid worker overseas • be part of a research team • be involved in working out/developing solutions (for) …
> **I enjoy:** the thrill of doing something difficult/exhausting/strenuous • the buzz of interacting with others • new challenges • creating new types of music/art • the excitement of discovering/exploring new places • the satisfaction of helping other people/improving people's lives/living standards
> **I had to:** study for many years • acquire the knowledge and skills to be able to … • experiment with different approaches • train to become fit enough to … • practise for years to gain the experience/skills to be able to … • learn about the needs of the people/society I wanted to help

_____
_____
_____
_____
_____
_____
_____
_____

b Describe what, in your view, should be the three highest priorities of your generation. Explain why you would choose these. You may find the vocabulary in the box helpful.

> *Firstly, … • I would choose … as my first priority • I agreed with the group that … • I take the view that … • I think/feel that … • My point is (that) … • My second priority is … • In my view, … • Secondly/Thirdly, …*

_____
_____
_____
_____
_____
_____
_____

▶ S13: The stages of writing, WB pp. 72–73

Words in Context

Teen years, in-between years

Look at 'Words in Context' (SB p. 12) again and fill in the empty boxes in the following wordlist.
In the 'Memory Support' box you can either …
- put the word or phrase in a sentence, or
- think of words belonging to the same family, or
- write down other collocations.

You can download this wordlist and edit it on your computer here:

Webcode starwb-01

Word/Phrase	Memory support	German
a stage of life	Adulthood is a stage of life when a person is usually at their peak level of performance.	
a period of transition	Because adolescence is a period of transition from childhood to adulthood, teenagers often feel unsure of themselves.	
(to) assert yourself	WORD FAMILY:	sich durchsetzen, sich behaupten
	OTHER COLLOCATIONS: a key/vital/major role	eine aktive Rolle spielen
(to) come of age	In the past adolescents came of age at 21, but nowadays in most countries it's 18.	
(to) have rights and responsibilities	You need to become aware of the rights and responsibilities you have as an adult.	
(to) gain acceptance	Many young people try to gain acceptance from their own peer group.	
a peer group		eine Peergroup (*Gruppe etwa Gleichaltriger*)
peer pressure	For many teenagers, peer pressure is much more important than the influence of their parents or teachers.	
self-confident		selbstbewusst
self-conscious		befangen, gehemmt
popularity	She didn't increase her popularity when she started making fun of their friends.	

The Time of Your Life   Chapter 1

1 Words in Context

Word/Phrase	Memory support	German
	WORD FAMILY: (to) expose – exposure – exposé – exposition	Einflüssen ausgesetzt sein
under pressure	**OTHER COLLOCATIONS:**	unter Druck
(to) meet your parents' expectations	Many children find it difficult to meet their parents' expectations.	
	OTHER COLLOCATIONS: (to) gain access to sth. – (to) gain time/ground – (to) gain experience/confidence/strength	einen Studienplatz bekommen, an einer Universität (zum Studium) zugelassen werden
(to) give serious consideration to one's future		sich ernsthaft mit seiner Zukunft befassen, ernsthaft über die eigene Zukunft nachdenken
	WORD FAMILY: conformity – conformist	sich dem Anpassungsdruck beugen/unterwerfen
(to) strive hard	We are striving hard to become the best in our field.	
	OTHER COLLOCATIONS: (to) reach a level/speed/stage/target – (to) reach a conclusion/decision/compromise	die persönlichen/selbst gesteckten Ziele erreichen
(to) take risks		Risiken eingehen, etwas riskieren
(to) test your limits	Athletes need to test their limits if they want to improve their performance.	
a role model		ein Vorbild
(to) tend to experiment	Most people tend to experiment with different approaches when they start work.	
(to) rebel against sth. [rɪˈbel]	**WORD FAMILY:**	sich gegen etwas auflehnen
provocative [prəˈvɒkətɪv ☆ prəˈvɑːkətɪv]		provozierend, anstößig, (sexuell auch) aufreizend
(to) yearn for security	He rebelled against his parents, but he really yearned for security and a stable family life.	

Teen years, in-between years   1

2 Which words, which phrases?   SB WiC ◄

Which words or phrases from 'Words in Context' fit the situations below. The lines show the number of letters.

1 To g_ _ _ _ a_ _ _ _ _ _ _ _ _ _ _ within a particular group of people you often have to prove that you're the right sort of person for that group.

2 I've not yet been e_ _ _ _ _ _ _ _ t_ these sort of i_ _ _ _ _ _ _ _ _ _ before, so I'm not sure how to deal with them.

3 The problem with p_ _ _ _ p_ _ _ _ _ _ _ _ is that it sometimes forces you to do things which you don't really want to do.

4 Whatever s_ _ _ _ _ o_ l_ _ _ _ you happen to be in, you'll find that there will always be problems: nothing is ever plain sailing.

5 An adult h_ _ greater r_ _ _ _ _ _ a_ _

r_ _ _ _ _ _ _ _ _ _ _ _ _ _ _ _ than a teenager does.

6 You often have to t_ _ _ _ r_ _ _ _ _ if you want to r_ _ _ _ _ y_ _ _

p_ _ _ _ _ _ _ _ g_ _ _ _ .

7 As she got older, she decided to p_ _ _ _ an a_ _ _ _ _ _ _ r_ _ _ _ in local politics and stood for election to the local council.

8 Adolescence is considered a p_ _ _ _ _ _ o_ t_ _ _ _ _ _ _ _ _ _ between childhood and adulthood.

3 Saying it, spelling it   SB WiC ◄

a Pronounce these words from 'Words in Context', writing down the correct spelling.

1 [əˈsɜːt] _____   5 [ɪksˈperɪmənt] _____

2 [rɪˈbel] (v) _____   6 [ˌselfˈkɒnfɪdənt] _____

3 [kənˈfɔːm] _____   7 [prəˈvɒkətɪv] _____

4 [jɜːn] _____

b Do the same with these related words.

1 [ˈrebl] (n) _____   3 [ˌkɒnfɪˈdenʃl] _____

2 [ɪksˌperɪmənˈteɪʃn] _____   4 [ˌprɒvəˈkeɪʃn] _____

4 What do you call ... ?   SB WiC ◄

Without looking at SB p. 12, give the answer to these questions.

What do you call ...

1 ... a group of people with the same age or same social status as you?

4 ... it when you look very carefully at what you are going to do with your life?

2 ... a person who other people try to copy because they admire this person?

5 ... it when you have the feeling of being forced to do sth.?

3 ... it when you reach the age where you have an adult's rights and responsibilities?

6 ... the state of being liked by many people?

The Time of Your Life   Chapter 1   7

Part A

You can download the audio file and transcript here:
Webcode starwb-02

Hopes, fears and realities

5 Listening comprehension: Work to live or live to work?   SB A1 ◀

Kerry Eustice of the *Guardian* is interviewing Phil Bolton, a career coach at *Escape the City*, an online platform supporting corporate professionals who want to do something different with their working lives. They are comparing graduate employees' current expectations of their jobs with those described in an *Observer* article in 2008. The podcast was made in 2011.

a Listening for gist: Listen to the interview once only, just for gist. Then answer this question: What approach to work does Phil recommend? Tick the correct box.
    a ☐ He recommends working to live.
    b ☐ He says people should live to work.
    c ☐ He remains neutral.

b Listening for detail: Now listen again for detail and tick the correct answer:
1. What attitude was most popular among graduates in 2008, before the 2008 financial crisis?
    a ☐ They were more interested in fulfilment, satisfaction and enjoyment.
    b ☐ Their main interest was in earning a good salary.
    c ☐ They wanted to have a responsible position in the companies they worked for.

2. How had this changed by 2011? Tick the correct answer.
    a ☐ 30%–40% wanted to change jobs.
    b ☐ 30%–40% wanted any sort of job.
    c ☐ 13%–14% wanted to have a new job.

3. How do Kerry and Phil describe the attitude to jobs in their parents' generation? Tick the correct answer.
    a ☐ They were less interested in their children's education, more in surviving.
    b ☐ They wanted to earn big salaries to support themselves, pay the rent and put their children through school and university.
    c ☐ For them, quality of life was the main thing.

4. What attitude does Phil see emerging among young people and older adults?
_____
_____
_____

▶ S1: Listening for information, WB pp. 56–57

6 Health and illness   SB A4 ◀

Complete the following sentences using health and illness words and phrases from **A4** in the SB (p. 18). Each line represents one word.

1. Mrs Dawson is one of the p_____ at the Wexner Medical Center.

2. She has to take tablets every day because of her high b_____ p_____.

3. She's also been walking around on c_____ since she had a car accident.

4. She injured one of the vertebrae in her l_____ b_____.

5. The i_____ to her spleen were so great that the s_____ had to remove it.

6. As her condition was still critical, after the operation, she was taken straight to i_____ c_____.

7. After six weeks in hospital, she needed to go for r_____.

Hopes, fears and realities

7 About Dave and Jenny SB A4 ◀

Use the cues below to form sentences about two other patients, Dave and Jenny. The first one has been done for you. Take special care with the tenses.

1 Dave / want / to be / a surgeon / since / he / be / a child
   Dave has wanted to be a surgeon since he was a child.

2 Dave / spend / months in hospital / since / he / have / the accident
   _____

3 He / walk / on crutches / since / his leg / be amputated
   _____

4 He / have / a passion for medicine / since / he / be / at elementary school
   _____

5 Since / the nurse / take / Jenny's crutches / away, / she / be able to / walk / on her own
   _____

6 Since / she / discuss / the options / with her doctors, / she / decide / to study medicine
   _____

7 Since / she / talk / to her doctors, / she / have / a better idea / of the difficulties
   _____

▶ L4: Present perfect and simple past, SB p. 167

FOCUS ON LANGUAGE — PRONUNCIATION

8 Playing with sounds and letters SB A6 ◀

a Linking: Try pronouncing these phrases.

1 a nawesome experience
2 they fee lunder pressure
3 they see kacceptance
4 play a nactive role

Say the following phrases, then write them out in normal spelling.

5 a bagof chips _____
6 it cause da nexplosion _____
7 he gaze dinto her eyes _____
8 I caught a cabin town _____

> **TIP**
> In German a short pause (the 'glottal stop') is often used before stressed vowels, e.g. in 'iss einen Apfel'. In English, syllables are linked without any pause between them. So *eat an apple* actually sounds like *eatanapple*.
> This method can also be used to help to pronounce voiced consonants correctly.

b A misunderstanding: At an international conference, a German speaker stressed that the Russian economy had to reach the same level as that of the West. He called this the 'ketchup strategy'. What did he mean, and why did he make this pronunciation mistake?

_____
_____

c Comparing the stress: Underline the stressed syllables in the words below.

1 continue – continuity
2 curious – curiosity
3 mystery – mysterious
4 optimist – optimistic
5 person – personality
6 trauma – traumatic

7 Now look up the stress of these words in a dictionary:
   unhappy – unnecessary – unfriendly – uninjured – uninformed – uninteresting

8 What do you notice about the stress?
   _____

> **TIP**
> The position of the stress in English words derived from foreign languages varies. Some suffixes, e.g. *-ic(al)*, *-ious* and *-ity* change the stress. Others, e.g. *-ize*, *-ous*, do not.

The Time of Your Life — Chapter 1

Part B

Spread your wings

9 Greater awareness: gerunds and infinitives   SB B2

a Choose the correct alternatives to complete the following sentences. The first six are taken from the text of SB **B2** (pp. 22–23). Tick the correct box.

1 Her father's hints happened … with the young Ford salesman's fourth proposal of marriage.
  a ☐ coinciding
  b ☐ to coincide
  c ☐ to coinciding

2 She tried to act as if she were waiting for somebody … on the next bus.
  a ☐ to be coming in
  b ☐ for coming in
  c ☐ to come in

3 It was time for her to think about … something with her life.
  a ☐ to do
  b ☐ doing
  c ☐ to be doing

4 She wanted … a movie magazine tragedy.
  a ☐ her life being
  b ☐ her life to be
  c ☐ that her life is

5 He was tired … his daughter sit around the house all the time.
  a ☐ of watching
  b ☐ to watch
  c ☐ of to watch

6 She left the house after getting out of …
  a ☐ to do the dishes.
  b ☐ do the dishes.
  c ☐ doing the dishes.

7 She wasn't used … alone at the bus station at night.
  a ☐ to sitting
  b ☐ to sit
  c ☐ sitting

8 She was looking forward …
  a ☐ to get back home.
  b ☐ for getting back home.
  c ☐ to getting back home.

▶ L12: The gerund, SB pp. 175–176

b Now fill in the gaps in the text below with the correct form of the verb, using either the gerund or the infinitive. Add the correct preposition where necessary.

When I was about six or seven I used _____¹ (say) that I wanted _____² (be) a surgeon when I grew up, but nowadays I'm not so sure. I dislike _____³ (see) blood, so lots of people have recommended _____⁴ (change) my career plans. Instead I'm now planning _____⁵ (study) biochemistry. My doctor has advised me _____⁶ (avoid) _____⁷ (choose) a job where I'm outside all day. I suffer from severe hay fever, so any job that involves _____⁸ (be) outside a lot is not an option. Since I enjoy _____⁹ (read), a desk job would suit me fine, but I wouldn't mind _____¹⁰ (work) in a lab, either. I'd like _____¹¹ (find) a well-paid job if I can, but the possibility _____¹² (get) one if I work in an office or lab is not very realistic. Who knows, maybe I'll just meet somebody rich?

Spread your wings

10 Greater awareness: images in a text — SB B2

a Authors of both fiction and non-fiction use images, e.g. similes and metaphors, to make their texts more interesting. Look again at SB **B2** (pp. 22–23) and find the images that complete the following sentences:

1 Movie magazines were _____

2 She studied [movie magazines] _____

3 Time was running out _____

4 [She sat] reading movie _____

5 [The old people's] suitcase was _____

6 [She] could have rented herself out _____

b **CHALLENGE** What does the author mean by these images? Explain three of them.

FOCUS ON SKILLS WRITING
Planning your writing

11 Creating an outline — SB B3

Practise organizing the outline of an essay dealing with the role of Hollywood in general, 'Hollywood the Dream Factory'. Arrange the jumbled ideas below according to the three main ideas of the essay. Work out first which are the main ideas.

- people identify with the characters in a film
- films motivate people, giving them a model to look up to and follow
- positive and negative effects
- dreams give people a goal to aim for
- how Hollywood uses people's dreams
- Hollywood enables people to escape from their everyday lives
- Hollywood films broaden people's horizons
- dreams provide people with strength
- films mislead people because movie plots are often unrealistic
- why people need dreams

Main idea 1: _____

   a) _____

   b) _____

Main idea 2: _____

   a) _____

   b) _____

   c) _____

Main idea 3: _____

   a) _____

   b) _____

▶ S13: The stages of writing, WB pp. 72–73

1 Part B

12 Using a bilingual dictionary SB B4

The grammatical information, pronunciation and usage notes in a bilingual dictionary can all help you to use the words you find correctly. Look at the dictionary entries for four terms from text **B4** in the SB (p. 26), then answer the questions below.

eigen 1 my, your, etc. own ◊ *Ich habe es mit eigenen Augen gesehen.* I saw it with my own eyes. ◊ *Das ist deine eigene Schuld!* It's your own fault! ◊ *auf eigene Verantwortung* at your own risk ◊ *Sie sollen sich ihre eigene Meinung bilden.* They should form their own opinions. ◊ *Sie möchte ein eigenes Auto.* She would like a car of her own. ◊ *ein Zimmer mit eigenem Bad* a room with a private bathroom

> Vorsicht: **Own** wird ohne Artikel verwendet: ◊ *a house of your own/your own house.* Man kann nicht sagen: „an own house".

2 (*separat*) separate ◊ *Die Galerie hat einen eigenen Eingang.* There is a separate entrance for the gallery. **3** (*charakteristisch*) characteristic ◊ *mit der ihm eigenen Direktheit* with characteristic directness ◊ *Diese sarkastische Art war ihr eigen.* This sarcastic manner was typical of her. ◊ *Die Landschaft hat ihren eigenen Reiz.* The countryside has its own special charm. **4** (*penibel*) particular ◊ *In Bezug auf Sauberkeit ist er sehr eigen.* He is very particular about cleanliness. ⓘ *Für andere Ausdrücke mit* **eigen** *siehe die Einträge für die entsprechenden Nomina etc.* **Auf eigenen Beinen stehen** *z. B. steht unter* **Bein**.

Vernunft 1 reason; (*gesunder Menschenverstand*) common sense **2 mit ~** sensibly **3 politische, ökonomische etc. ~** political, economic, etc. sense ◊ *Das geht gegen die wirtschaftliche Vernunft.* It does not make economic sense. IDM **Vernunft annehmen** see* **sense** *Wann wird er endlich Vernunft annehmen?* When will he finally see sense? ◊ *Nimm doch endlich Vernunft an und geh zum Arzt!* Just be sensible and go to the doctor. **jdm Vernunft beibringen** make* sb see reason **zur Vernunft kommen** come* to your senses

Abiturient(in) (*vor dem Abitur*) ≈ A level student/student taking Highers, (*AmE*) ≈ student taking the high-school diploma; (*mit Abitur*) ≈ student who has taken A levels/the high-school diploma ⓘ *Hinweis bei* ABITUR

mutig brave (*Adv* bravely) courageous (*Adv* courageously) ◊ *Du bist vom obersten Brett gesprungen? Mutig, mutig!* You jumped off the top board? That was brave! ◊ *eine mutige Antwort* a courageous answer

> „Mutig" wird mit **brave** übersetzt, wenn es darum geht, dass jemand (oft in gefährlichen Situationen) Tapferkeit beweist bzw. etwas tapfer durchsteht. **Courageous** wird benutzt, wenn es sich um (moralische) Entscheidungen etc. handelt, in denen man Mut beweist.

Source: *Das große Oxford Wörterbuch*, 2009

1 'eigenes Haus' (l. 3): Of course, 'eigen' is *own*, and 'Haus' is usually *house*, but check the usage note on 'eigen' in the dictionary. What does it say?

_____

_____

2 'Generation Ratio' (l. 3): Which of the following phrases would you choose to translate this into English? Before you decide, check the word *ratio*.

generation ratio – our generation – this generation – the ratio generation

3 'Sicher, Vernunft ist eine Tugend.' (l. 5): The dictionary gives three main translations – *reason, common sense, sense*. Sometimes, however, it is better not to stick too closely to German constructions, i.e. a literal translation. For example, German often uses nouns where English uses verbs. Which of the following options sound(s) most natural? More than one may be correct.
   a ☐ Of course, reason is a virtue.
   b ☐ Of course, being sensible is a virtue.
   c ☐ Of course, common sense is a virtue.
   d ☐ Of course, sense is a virtue.

4 'Abiturienten' (l. 13): How would you translate this?
   a ☐ Use the dictionary translations *A level students, students taking the high-school diploma.*
   b ☐ Choose a more general word so that it refers to anybody leaving school, e.g. *school leavers*.
   c ☐ Use a less specific word, e.g. *students*.

Explain the reasons for your choice.

_____

5 'Sturm und Drang' (l. 17): Which English option would you choose in this context? Why?

storm and stress – storm and desire – emotions

_____

_____

_____

6 'die Mutigen' (l. 27): The dictionary gives two main English alternatives. What are they and what's the difference? Which would you choose in this context?

_____

_____

_____

_____

▶ S25: Using a dictionary, WB pp. 86–89

Spread your wings

13 Reporting what people said

SB B4 ◀

a Several classmates are talking about what they want to do when they leave school. Report what they say, using indirect speech and the verbs in the box. Highlight the verb of saying and underline the verb in indirect speech, as shown in the example.

> add • admit • advise • ask • explain • promise • say • stress • suggest • tell • warn

Brian: I want to become a lawyer.

Layla: My ambition is to become a vet. I love looking after animals.

Geoff: I'm thinking of doing Latin and Ancient Greek at uni.

Becky: I've always wanted to be a journalist, but now I'm not so sure.

Andrew: I'm going to train to be a teacher. I think teaching kids will be great.

Paula: Geoff, do you really think it's a good idea to do Classics? You may not get a job afterwards.

Chris: Becky, be careful. A lot of newspapers are closing. Why don't you try something else?

Karen: Can anybody give me some advice? I haven't a clue what to do later.

Brian said that he wanted to become a lawyer.

TIP

When reporting direct speech, i.e. by using indirect speech, you often need to change the tenses of the original text as well as the pronouns. Remember also to vary the vocabulary – don't always use *say* or *tell*.

► L10: Indirect speech, SB p. 174
► L21: Verbs of reporting, SB p. 184

b Matthias is writing a letter to the form teacher at the school where he spent a year in Scotland. He got to know his form teacher quite well, and they have kept in touch. In his letter he's telling Mr Macpherson about a talk he recently listened to at school. This is what the speaker said:

> Ladies and gentlemen, I want to talk to you today about your future. You may be wondering what a 50-year-old businessman can tell you that would be relevant to your lives. Well, remember that I was your age once. In 1985 I was working as a cub reporter in my home country, South Africa. I was a pretty conventional sort of guy from the white suburbs. My life changed dramatically when I met a stunning black girl, Miriam, from one of the townships. Under apartheid it was illegal, but we started going out regularly. My parents and friends were outraged when they found out. I ignored their protests and we were arrested. I lost my job and went through hell. Despite all the hardship, I've never regretted not taking the easy, conventional route. I set up my own computer software business, which is doing well. We've got three fantastic kids. Like South Africa, we have had our ups and downs, but Miriam and me are still together. And since apartheid was abolished, even my parents have gradually come round to accepting my mixed-race family. So my advice is: don't be conventional. Follow your heart. It won't make your lives easier, but I promise you that it will make them more interesting.

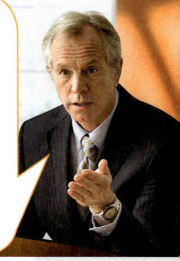

CHALLENGE Continue Matthias's letter below, putting the direct speech into indirect speech. Highlight the verbs of saying or asking, and underline the verbs in indirect speech, as shown in the example.

Dear Mr Macpherson,
You will probably remember that when I was at Inverness Academy we talked quite a lot about my future plans. Well, recently we had a few people coming to talk to us about the choices open to us after school and one of them made me think, although he didn't tell us much about actual careers. He began by saying that he wanted to talk to us about our future.

TIPS

1 If it is clear that a text involves indirect speech the past simple of direct speech often remains unchanged, to avoid using the past perfect each time. This is very common in long pieces of indirect speech.
2 If the facts being reported are still true, it is also possible to keep the original tense although the verb of saying is in the past simple, e.g. *He said that his friend lives/lived in Canada.*
3 In long pieces of indirect speech we often remind the reader or listener that the text is still indirect speech by adding a verb of saying or reporting.

The Time of Your Life — Chapter 1

1 Part B

14 CHALLENGE ▸ Giving a short talk

Imagine you are an exchange student abroad. You've been asked by your teacher to give a short talk about the hopes, fears and problems of young people in Germany. Write about 500 words. The checklist below will help you.

☐ Have you structured your talk?
☐ Does the talk have an introduction, body and conclusion?
☐ Is the introduction interesting? (Does is contain an anecdote, joke, quotation or surprising fact?)
☐ Is the body of the talk split into main ideas? (An easy structure would be: 1) hopes, 2) fears, 3) problems. When you write them, put them in separate paragraphs.)
☐ Do you give evidence or examples to support what you say?
☐ Have you checked the pronunciation of important words?
☐ Does your conclusion leave your audience with a clear idea of your most important points?
☐ If possible, your conclusion should be interesting or dramatic. Is it?

▸ S10: Giving a presentation, WB p. 69

15 Difficult choices

a Fill in the gaps with suitable words or phrases from the box below.

> a choice • an alternative • (to) choose this option • (to) decide in favour of this •
> (to) decide against sth. • (to) have freedom of choice • (to) have the freedom/right to choose
> • (to) opt for sth. • (to) reject sth.

Arthur was the sort of person who liked to have _____1 between two options. His problem was that he could never make up his mind. When he was faced with an _____2, he could never _____3 of the one option, because that would mean _____4 against the other one. He saw the advantages of both and felt that it was wrong to _____5 any option which had so many good sides to it. So he _____6 for neither one nor the other. Later, in his thirties, he often complained that freedom was a curse rather than a blessing, but his friends only smiled sadly about a man who had never learned to make _____7.

b Choose two of the following situations and then decide which alternative (**a** or **b**) you would prefer. Explain why you made these choices. The phrases you used in **a** will help you.

1
a You have a well-paid but routine job with good chances of promotion.
b You have a job with average pay but a lot of variety in the types of work you do.

2
a Your partner is ordinary but reliable and is easy to get on with.
b Your partner is good looking and exciting but is not always loyal to you.

3
a You've got two children, a boy and a girl, who do not dominate your life and leave you some time for hobbies and outside interests.
b You've got a large family of 4–6 children who take up most of your time and are lots of fun, but you have no time for your hobbies.

4
a You have friends who do lots of exciting things but don't always have much time for you.
b Your friends are dependable – you know you can count on them when you're in difficulties.

▸ S13: The stages of writing, WB pp. 72–73

Chapter 1 The Time of Your Life

Focus on Literature

Narrative Prose – the Novel

1 Gathering information SB A ◄

The following extract is from the beginning of the novel *iBoy* by Kevin Brooks.

▶ S7: Reading and analysing narrative prose, WB pp. 61–63

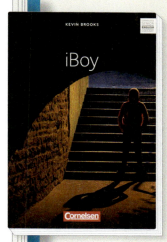

The mobile phone that shattered my skull was a 32GB iPhone 3GS. It weighed 135g, measured 115.5mm x 62.1mm x 12.3mm, and at the time of impact it was travelling at approximately 77mph. Of course, I didn't know any of this at the time. All I knew at the time, the only thing I was vaguely aware of, was a small black object hurtling down through the afternoon sky towards me, and then …

5 CRACK!

A momentary flash of blinding pain …

And then nothing.

Twenty minutes earlier, everything had been perfectly normal. It was Friday 5 March, and the streets were still mushy with the remains of last week's snow. I'd left school at the usual time, just gone three
10 thirty, and I'd started the walk back home feeling pretty much the same as I always felt. Kind of OK, but not great. Alone, but not lonely. A bit down about things, but not really worried about anything in particular. I was just my perfectly normal ordinary self. I was Tom Harvey, a sixteen-year-old kid from South London. I had no major problems, no secrets, no terrors, no vices, no nightmares, no special talents … I had no story to tell. I was just a kid, that's all. I had my hopes and dreams, of course,
15 just like everyone else. But that's all they were – hopes and dreams.

And I suppose one of those hopes, one of those dreams, was the girl I was thinking about as I made my way along the High Street, then down Crow Town, the estate where I lived (its official name is the Crow Lane Estate, but everyone calls it Crow Town).

The girl's name was Lucy Walker.

20 I'd known Lucy for years, since we were both little kids and we used to live next door to each other. Her mum used to babysit for my gran sometimes, and my gran would babysit for her, and then later on, when we were both a bit older, me and Lucy used to spend a lot of time playing together – in each other's flats, in the corridors, in the lifts, on the swings and stuff at the kids' playground on the estate. Lucy didn't live next door to me any more, but she was still in the same tower block (Compton House),
25 just a few floors up, and I still knew her quite well. I'd see her at school sometimes, and occasionally we'd walk back home together, and every now and then I'd go round to her place and hang around for a while, or she'd come over to mine …

But we didn't play on the swings together any more.

And I kind of missed that.

30 I missed a lot about Lucy Walker.

So it'd been kind of nice when she'd come up to me in the school playground earlier that day and asked if I could come round to her place after school.

'I need to talk to you about something,' she'd said. […]

From: Kevin Brooks, *iBoy*, London: Penguin UK, 2010

1 **skull** the bone protecting your brain
13 **vices** *here:* bad habits
17 **estate** large collection of houses or flats

a While reading, make notes on what kind of boy the narrator is: (name, age, where he lives, his family, his friends, …).

b Write in one sentence what happened to him that afternoon.

c The first chapter of the novel ends with another, shorter description of the incident, and the last words are: 'The end of normality.' What do you expect the novel to be about, taking into consideration the title *iBoy*?

▶ S22: Making and taking notes, WB p. 84

LIT Narrative Prose – the Novel

2 Looking at language   SB A

a Read the extract from *iBoy* again and underline the phrase 'kind of' each time it is used. Re-write the sentences replacing 'kind of' with a less colloquial expression each time.

b In lines 20–27 the narrator tells us about how things used to be between himself and Lucy. Find the expression that he uses as a synonym for 'used to'.

c Translate the last two lines of the passage, concentrating on the underlined phrases.

> <u>I'd see</u> her at school sometimes, and <u>occasionally we'd walk</u> back home together, and every now and <u>then I'd go</u> round to her place and hang around for a while, or <u>she'd come</u> over to mine …

3 What's going to happen?   SB B/C

> The narrator, Tom, has found out that he has supernatural powers because some bits of the iPhone are permanently lodged in his brain. On the one hand, he has access to anything on the internet, so he found out that his friend Lucy was raped on the afternoon he was supposed to see her; on the other hand, he is able to direct electric shock-waves to people and things with his hands. He is obsessed with the idea of revenge.

The estate was unusually quiet as I crossed the stretch of grass between Compton House and Crow Lane. The towers, the streets, the empty black sky … everything was bathed in that dead-of-night silence that makes you feel like you're the only living thing in the world.

The night was cold. My breath was misting in the air, my hands were icy, and I could feel the soft crunch of frost beneath my feet. 5

But I didn't care.

Hot or cold … it didn't make any difference to me. I was in that state of controlled brutality again – in control of being out of control – and the only thing I could feel was an overriding and irresistible sense of purpose. Get there, find them, find him … get there, find them, find him … get there, find them, find him … 10

I walked on – across the grass, through the gate in the railings, along Crow Lane – and as I approached the entrance to Baldwin House, the sound of voices began to break through the darkened silence. Raised voices, laughter, the soft rumble of an idling car engine …

I couldn't see anyone yet, but it wasn't hard to guess what kind of people the voices belonged to – I mean, they were hanging around Baldwin House at quarter to four in the morning … they weren't 15 going to be choir boys, were they?

I heard the car engine revving, a dog snarling, another shout of laughter, and then – as I turned off Crow Lane and into the square around Baldwin House – I saw them: half a dozen or so gang kids, all in hoods and caps, hanging around a VW Golf in front of the tower block doors. A skinny Doberman and a Staff with a spiked collar were skulking around the car, neither of them on leads. A couple of 20 the kids were quite young – twelve or thirteen – but most of them were about seventeen or eighteen.

I didn't recognize any of them.

The dogs noticed me first, and as they both started running at me, barking and snarling, the kids all stopped whatever it was they'd been doing and turned to see what was happening. They saw me walking towards them – my skin shimmering, my hooded face a pale glow of radiating light – and 25 they watched, confused, as the two dogs suddenly sensed something about me that scared the shit out of them. They skidded to a halt about two metres away from me, their ears flat, their tails between their legs, and then they both sloped off, whimpering quietly.

From: Kevin Brooks, *iBoy*, London: Penguin UK, 2010

13 **idling** *(of an engine)* im Leerlauf
17 **revving** turning faster, as if to accelerate
19/20 **Doberman, Staff** (= **Staffordshire bull terrier**) breeds of aggressive dogs, often used as guard dogs and sometimes for illegal dogfights
23 **snarl** make an ugly deep noise in your throat
27 **skid** slide along the ground
28 **slope off** run away quietly, as if not wanting to be seen

The extract above is also from the novel *iBoy*.

a Imagine someone has made a video of the scene. Describe what you would see and hear in the video in as much detail as possible, using adjectives and participles from the text.

b There is not much action in the extract, but there is a strong feeling that something is going to happen soon. Write how you think the chapter will continue. Use intelligent guesswork based on what you already know and the atmosphere in the scene you have just described.

Communicating in the Digital Age 2

Lead-in

1 Which is better?   SB L-i ◀

a Compare traditional TV with an internet video platform. What, in your view, are the advantages and disadvantages of the two types of media? Make notes in the table below.

> a lot of / not much / no feedback • anonymous • a wide variety of • centralized • dependent on • DSL download speed • for commercial purposes • upload speed • greater/less variety • interactive • quality of the sound and picture • response • to click on sth. • to provide/give feedback • to respond • to vary • user profiling

	TV	Internet video platform
advantages		
disadvantages		

b Now use the phrases from the box below to explain in greater detail what you noted down in the table above. 📝

> Good?   an advantage of • a good point about • a good side to • a useful/positive effect of
> Bad?   a disadvantage of • a downside to • a drawback of • a negative effect of

▶ S13: The stages of writing, WB pp. 72–73

2 Communicating   SB L-i ◀

a Which form of communication from the box below is, in your view, most suitable for the situations 1–8? More than one answer may be correct.

> email • instant message • mobile phone • smartphone • speaking face-to-face • text message • voiceover IP, e.g. using Skype • social networking site

1 researching information during break at school   _____
2 talking to a friend in Australia   _____
3 talking to a friend while on the bus   _____
4 quick news update with friends while at home   _____
5 exchanging news and photos with friends   _____
6 writing to one friend, others can't see the message   _____
7 writing to a company for information   _____
8 talking to someone with maximum feedback   _____

b Describe one of these situations as an example and write a short statement saying what form of communication you would choose and why. 📝

Communicating in the Digital Age   Chapter 2

2 Words in Context

Keeping in touch in the 21st century

You can download this wordlist and edit it on your computer here:

 Webcode starwb-03

Look at 'Words in Context' (SB p. 38) again and fill in the empty boxes in the following wordlist. In the 'Memory support' box you can either …
- put the word or phrase in a sentence, or
- think of words belonging to the same family, or
- write down other collocations.

Word/Phrase	Memory support	German
(to) **use search engines**	We can use search engines to look for information on the world wide web.	
(to) **retrieve information**		Informationen abrufen
	You can upload your essay to the internet and make it available to other potential users.	Inhalte ins Internet hochladen/stellen
(to) **gain access to a global audience**	OTHER COLLOCATIONS: global warming/ban/approach/village worldwide/TV audience	
a contributor [kənˈtrɪbjətə]	WORD FAMILY:	ein Mitwirkender, ein Beitragender
a hand-held device	OTHER COLLOCATIONS: portable/marketing/labour-saving/water-saving device	
	Information nowadays is going portable, with smartphones and notebooks dominating.	tragbar/transportierbar/mobil werden
information available online		online verfügbare Informationen
(to) **access information** [ˈækses]	WORD FAMILY:	auf Informationen zugreifen, Informationen abfragen
a wireless connection	OTHER COLLOCATIONS:	eine drahtlose Verbindung
(to) **enhance the usefulness of** sth. [ɪnˈhɑːns ☆ ɪnˈhæns]	Apps can greatly enhance the usefulness of your smartphone.	
(to) **influence the way we do** sth.	Digital communications technology influences the way we communicate with each other.	

Chapter 2 — Communicating in the Digital Age

Words in Context 2

Word/Phrase	Memory support	German
text-based communication		textbasierte Kommunikation
social networking sites (SNS)		soziale Netzwerke
instant messages	Instant messages have greatly increased the speed of communication between individuals.	
(to) link people	WORD FAMILY:	Menschen verbinden
	Hiphop appeals mainly to a young audience – most older people prefer quieter music.	hauptsächlich junge Menschen ansprechen
(to) make new contacts		neue Kontakte knüpfen
(to) post photos/messages	OTHER COLLOCATIONS:	Fotos/Nachrichten posten
a false sense of security	The many safeguards of privacy of the individual in the Constitution can easily create a false sense of security in this age of cyberespionage.	
personal information		persönliche/private Informationen
the anonymity of cyberspace		die Anonymität des Cyberspace
a cyberbully	WORD FAMILY:	ein/e Cybermobber/in, ein/e Internetmobber/in
(to) torment sb.		jdn. quälen
a victim	WORD FAMILY: (to) victimize – victimless	
a legal consequence	What would the legal consequences of these internet threats to leading personalities be?	

Communicating in the Digital Age — Chapter 2

2 Words in Context

3 Collocations
SB WiC

Fill in the gaps in the following sentences so that the collocations from 'Words in Context' are complete. Then highlight the collocations.

Nowadays the internet is going _____¹: hand-held _____² are becoming more popular and users are no longer happy with being tied to a large computer or even to a less cumbersome laptop. They want to be able to _____³ information which is _____⁴ online or to _____⁵ content to the internet while they are on the move. All this has led to a rise in the use of _____⁶ communication to an extent that was unthinkable a decade ago. And using smartphones, people can not only _____⁷ messages, but also photos on the internet. Via this new technology we are _____⁸ together as never before, with all the advantages and disadvantages that that brings with it.

4 Familiar words, familiar phrases?
SB WiC

Which words or phrases from 'Words in Context' fit in the situations below? The lines show the number of letters.

1 I think we should treat c_____ the same way as any other bullies.
2 Many teenagers have become v_____ of bullying via the internet.
3 Use of digital media can lead to e_____ efficiency at the workplace.
4 Something's wrong with our w_____ c_____ – I can't seem to a_____ my incoming emails.
5 It's important to know how to r_____ information from the internet.
6 The fact that all their friends also use s_____ n_____ s_____ can easily give teenagers a f____ s_____ of s_____.

5 Crazy collocations
SB WiC

The collocations in the text below are confused. Write the highlighted words in their correct places so that the collocations from 'Words in Context' are correct and the text makes sense.

> *sites*
> Because so many people now use social networking messages, personal security is becoming widely available to outside sources. What is more, instant consequences mean that users can communicate much faster than in the past, which often results in them becoming less careful in their responses. The apparent anonymity of victims also gives them a false sense of information, which may lead some to misuse the new media, e.g. in cyberbullying, since they are unaware of the legal sites of their actions and think that they can torment their cyberspace without being punished.

20 | Chapter 2 | Communicating in the Digital Age

Part A

Changing ways of communicating

6 Cartoons

SB A1

a Describe the situation and people in the cartoons below. Use the vocabulary box to help you. You will need to answer the following questions:
- Who are the people shown in the cartoons?
- What are they doing?
- Where are they?

TIP
Take care with the pronunciation of *cartoon*. It's pronounced [kɑːˈtuːn].

"HI, I'M IN THE PRAM."

"IT'S ME, YOU IDIOT. I JUST DON'T WANT EVERYONE ELSE IN THIS RESTAURANT LOOKING MORE POPULAR THAN US."

▶ S29: Working with cartoons, WB p. 91

> a couple • a pushchair (BE) / a stroller (AE) • annoyed at • confused • depressed •
> in the foreground/background • mobile (phone) (BE) / cell phone (AE) • on the left/right •
> to look happy/unhappy • to sit at a table • to snow • to criticize sb./sth.

_____
_____
_____
_____
_____
_____
_____
_____

b What aspects of digital communication are the cartoonists making fun of?
_____
_____
_____

c Discuss how effective the cartoons are at getting their meaning across. Give reasons.

▶ S13: The stages of writing, WB pp. 72–73

Communicating in the Digital Age — Chapter 2

2 Part A

FOCUS ON SKILLS WRITING

7 Structuring a text and connecting ideas SB A3
Read through the text below.

Is texting good or bad?
Texting can be a good thing. You can communicate with all sorts of people anywhere you like. It's different to calling because you can text several people at once. Texting can be a very bad thing. One example is when you are at the multiplex and all you hear is people tapping the keys on their phones. Texting has its advantages. On the whole, in my view, there are more downsides. Of course, texting is often useful. We can communicate with people all over the world. It is easier than picking up the phone and calling. All we have to do is type 'I love you' to our mums instead of interrupting whatever she is doing by phoning her. Texting can be bad, in my opinion, because it may annoy the people around you if you are in a silent place like church or the cinema. It means that you lose many of the good sides of real communication, hearing someone's voice, and affects family communication – you are too busy texting your friends. The mum who you've just texted to say 'I love you' is the mum you ignore when you're texting. Texting can reduce the time spent on the family. Using your mobile or smartphone is good if you like hearing people's voices, but texting is simpler and is less difficult.

a What defects do you notice in the way the text was written? Tick the correct boxes.

☐ There is no clear structure. ☐ The writer does not give examples.

☐ There are not enough linking words. ☐ The paragraphing is illogical.

☐ There is no paragraphing. ☐ The heading does not make sense.

b Put the words and phrases in the box in the correct place in the table below.

> *also • although • another point is • as • as a result • at the same time • because • besides • but • consequently • despite • e.g. • finally • firstly • for example • however • in addition • in conclusion • in short • likewise • secondly • since • similarly • such as • therefore • thirdly • thus • to sum up • unlike • what is more*

▶ S13: The stages of writing, WB pp. 72–73

Functions	Examples
Organizing the text (listing points)	
Giving reasons	
Adding ideas	
Comparing thoughts	
Contrasting thoughts	
Giving examples	
Explaining results, consequences	
Summarizing, drawing conclusions	

c Now rewrite the text above, using the linking words from the table to improve the style and structure. ✎

22 Chapter 2 Communicating in the Digital Age

Changing ways of communicating

FOCUS ON SKILLS — LISTENING

SB A5 ◄

8 Listening strategies

You are going to listen to a podcast with Susan Greenfield and David Babbs, entitled 'Is the internet bringing out the best in us?'

a Before listening
Speculate what the text could be about. There are two people involved in the discussion. Will they be of the same opinion?

b Listening for gist
Read the following statements. While listening, tick the correct box.

a ☐ They are both trying to find ways of using the internet to the best advantage.

b ☐ One of them is worried about the effects of the internet, the other is more positive.

c ☐ One speaker is completely against the whole idea of using the internet, the other is very much in favour of it.

c Listening for detail
Before you listen for the second time, read the questions below. While listening take notes. After listening write out your answers.

1. Who are Susan and David?

2. What problems does Susan see if you only know someone via the internet?

3. What is David's attitude to the internet and face-to-face contact?

4. What does David think about Susan's attitude to social networks and the internet?

From: *Five-minute Debates*, www.theguardian.com, 15 July 2013

You can download the audio file and transcript here:

Webcode starwb-04

neuroscientist ['njʊərəʊsaɪəntɪst] person who studies the structure and function of the brain and nervous system
substantial large in amount, value or importance
inevitable unavoidable
by the same token for the same reasons
neurological [ˌnjʊərəˌlɒdʒɪkl] relating to nerves and the nervous system
38 Degrees social campaigning website
poppadom type of thin round crisp bread served with curry
like-minded thinking the same things, having the same attitudes
mind-set way of thinking

► S1: Listening for information, WB pp. 56–57
► S22: Making and taking notes, WB p. 84

Communicating in the Digital Age — Chapter 2

Part B

Parents, friends and strangers

9 How embarrassing!   SB B1 ◀

Make the text more lively by adding the adjectives in the box. In the text you will often need to turn the adjectives into adverbs.

> complete • entire • necessary • perfect • private • secret • simple • strong

> I understand why you don't want me to become your 'friend' on your social networking website. It is part of your life. It's important to have privacy, whether you're an adult or a teenager. So I agree with you when you say that you don't want to include me among your 'friends'. It's obvious anyway that as a mother I have a different role than your friends, and I believe in respecting my children's views. They're not always realistic, because sometimes you react too emotionally, but in this case I think you're right – it would be embarrassing to read all your secret thoughts, however innocent they may be.

10 Where cyberbullying happens   SB B2 ◀

▶ S28: Working with charts and graphs, WB p. 91

a What type of a diagram is this?

_____

b Describe where young Americans experience cyberbullying. The words and phrases in the box below will help you.

> according to the diagram • at 23% • it was experienced by • mentioned by • most frequently used place • popular • recorded by • respectively • the interviewees • this was followed by • those interviewed • to account for • user • venue

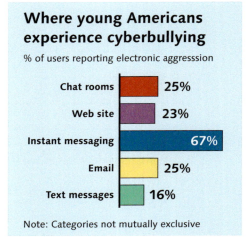

From: *Distribution of cyberbullying venues used by young people in the US*, Center for Disease Control

TIP

If you use the word *respectively*, note that it is used differently than *respektive* in German. We use it to compare two items which are listed, especially for statistics, and we put *respectively* after the statistics mentioned, e.g. *Germany and Britain have two of the largest populations in the EU, with 80 and 60 million people respectively*.

_____
_____
_____
_____
_____
_____
_____
_____
_____
_____

c Why do the percentages add up to more than 100%?

_____
_____

Parents, friends and strangers

11 Modifying the meaning

a Rewrite the highlighted parts of the sentences, using a modal verb or its substitutes, as shown in the example.

> **TIP**
> Modal verbs are used to modify the meaning of the main verb. They are often a problem for German learners because some English modals look like German ones, but are used differently. You may find it helpful to check modals in a grammar book before you tackle the following exercise.

1 It's advisable that people _People should_ try to protect themselves against an invasion of their privacy.

2 I need to _____ find out Jane's new email address.

3 We eventually managed to _____ skype with Danny. It was great to see him again.

4 It's essential that you _____ check whether anyone is watching when you type in your password in a public place.

5 It's not necessary for you to _____ have access to my Facebook account.

6 It's important that you're _____ careful what you publish on Facebook, as it's possible that what you write will be _____ used against you later, e.g. when applying for a job.

7 When using Wifi at a café, it's important that you remember _____ that the network will perhaps not be _____ encrypted, so you'll need to _____ check that you're using an SSL connection.

b Cross out the incorrect modal verb in these sentences, replacing it by the correct modal verb or substitute. There is one error in each sentence.

1 I mustn't buy a new tablet yet. My present one is only six months old.

2 When she left the room he could access her emails because she had left her PC running.

3 The new smartphone I want to get shall have some fantastic apps.

4 You mustn't 'friend' your parents if you don't want to. It's not necessary.

5 You shall try a different email provider if you keep having problems with this one.

6 Jenny and Tom could persuade their parents not to become their Facebook friends.

12 CHALLENGE Error spotting

Find and correct the errors in the sentences below. There are 3 preposition errors and 9 tense mistakes.

1 'How long do you have your new phone?'

2 'Only since a month. I've bought it in May. It's been in special offer.'

3 'Oh, how much was it costing?'

4 '£25. I was thinking that was a bargain.'

5 'I look around at the moment for a new provider. I've chosen this one because it was cheap, but I often don't get good reception by it and I think of switching. My old provider has been much better, so I may go back to them.'

Part B

13 The investigation

SB B4

The principal of Clover High School is investigating Carson's activities.
Use the clues below to reconstruct how the investigation went. Write the text of their conversation, taking special care with the tenses.

Principal: Carson, how long/you/know/Remy?
Carson: I guess, ever since/I/join/the school two years ago.
Principal: And when/you/start/to blackmail her?
Carson: Sir,/it/not be/blackmail. I/just/want/her help with the magazine/I/plan.
Principal: OK, so when/that/start?
Carson: Well, sir,/I/notice/a funny user name on the school website.
Principal: You/mean/this school's website?
Carson: Yes, sir,/I/mean/Clover High School's website. Anyway,/I/read/through the messages that/YearbookGirl69/post/on the website. I/suspect/that/Remy/might be/at the back of them, so/I/decide/to test my theory.
Principal: Why/be/it/so important to find out whether/Remy/hide/behind YearbookGirl69?
Carson: You see, sir,/I/have/problems recruiting students to contribute to the magazine, so/I/think/a little gentle pressure would help to persuade more people to join. Over the weekend/I/think/of ways to persuade her, so/I/message/YearbookGirl69 to test my theory.
Principal: Go on.
Carson: I/give/BadBoy2012 as my user name and/paste/a picture of Taylor Lautner's abs which/I/copy/off of the Internet.
Principal: And how/she/react?
Carson: She/take/the bait. When/I/sit/in the English class the next day,/I/have/a clear view of what/she/do/on her computer. I/message/her and/see/a window/pop up/on her PC screen. BadBoy2012/ask/YearbookGirl69 what/she/wear. Remy/reply/practically nothing. She/look/round the class to see if/anyone/watch/her, but/I/see/her/retrieve a photo from her documents and/attach/it. After school,/I/go/outside and/see/her. She/sit/on a bench on her own. I/hand/her a large envelope with the conversations between BadBoy2012 and YearbookGirl69. Then/I/take/one of the yellow flyers/you/find/and/give/it/to her.

▶ L1: The tenses: verb forms, SB p. 164

FOCUS ON LANGUAGE GRAMMAR
The simple form and the progressive form

14 What happened when you were doing that?

SB B5

Complete the following sentences with your own ideas, using the simple past or past progressive.

1 I was just texting my friend when _____
2 He was tweeting when _____
3 I was just getting my laptop out of my bag when _____
4 She was just flopping down on the sofa when _____
5 _____ when the teacher came in.
6 _____ when Dad asked me what I was doing.
7 _____ when she realized his mobile had been stolen.
8 _____ when Jenny asked me to come to her party.

▶ L5: Simple past and past progressive, SB p. 168

Parents, friends and strangers

15 Activities and states

Put the verbs in the box in the simple or progressive form in the gaps provided.

> change (2x) • go • fear • have • prefer • remain • say • seem • soar •
> take up • think (2x) • tweet

1 I _prefer_ _____ texting to phoning.

2 Social media _____ more of our time nowadays.

3 We _____ personal information should _____ anonymous.

4 I _____ on my social networking site twice a week.

5 There is no doubt that behaviour patterns _____ at the moment.

6 The government _____ that the costs of sustainable energy _____ .

7 She never _____ time to talk to me – she _____ all the time!

8 We _____ of buying a tablet PC, but then we _____ our minds.

9 Sternberg, who is a linguist, _____ that students increasingly _____ to be having trouble with the basics of direct communication.

16 CHALLENGE Nowhere to hide

You've just read an English text on the internet about cyberbullying. Summarize the text below in German for a friend.

Cyberbullying vs. traditional bullying

There are several differences between cyberbullying and traditional bullying. Unlike traditional bullying, electronic bullies do not need to reveal their identities, because they can use pseudonyms in chat rooms or instant messaging programs to hide their true identity. This also means that their behaviour as bullies can become more radical, as they are less limited by social conventions. In addition, the bullying is psychological rather than a use of physical violence, so that the bully tends to think of it as being less harmful. It's only words, and 'sticks and stones may break my bones, but calling names won't hurt me', as the old saying goes.

Secondly, in many cases the victim finds it difficult to avoid cyberbullying. Whereas in traditional bullying students who are being bullied can at least escape the bullying when they get home, cyberbullies can misuse people's dependence on mobile phones to gain access to the mobile phone user at home by phone calls or text messages. Changing the email address or avoiding specific chat rooms are only a partial solution, because some cyberbullies harm their victims by posting photos or untrue information about their victims on the internet. Once these have spread they are very difficult to remove.

Thirdly, there is no supervision of hate emails or text messages. Only where chat rooms are observed regularly by chat hosts is some form of check possible, enabling the chat host to evict cyberbullies. However, chat rooms only make up a small part of the problem, with instant messaging, emails and text messages taking the lion's share of cyberbullying venues.

▶ S21: Mediation of written and oral texts, WB pp. 81–83

Focus on Literature

▶ S7: Reading and analysing narrative prose, WB pp. 61–63

Narrative Prose – the Short Story

1 How may I help you?   SB A ◀

The narrator of the short story *Debbie's Call* (SB pp. 56–57) says that her friends make fun of her for using typical call-centre phrases in her private telephone conversations with them.
Below are the phrases she quotes herself using. How would you say these phrases in a private conversation?

1 'Hello, I'm Debbie. Thank you for calling. How may I help you?
_____

2 Can I be of any other assistance?
_____

3 Thank you for your patience.
_____

4 Feel free to call me with further queries.
_____

2 What does the narrator tell us?   SB B ◀

The following extract is the beginning of a short story by the Canadian author Alice Munro, who was awarded the Nobel Prize in Literature in 2013.

Alice Munro

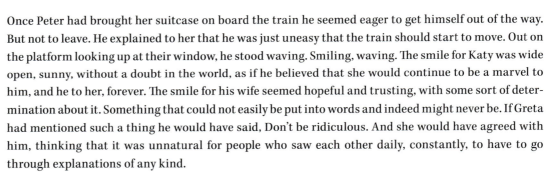

Once Peter had brought her suitcase on board the train he seemed eager to get himself out of the way. But not to leave. He explained to her that he was just uneasy that the train should start to move. Out on the platform looking up at their window, he stood waving. Smiling, waving. The smile for Katy was wide open, sunny, without a doubt in the world, as if he believed that she would continue to be a marvel to him, and he to her, forever. The smile for his wife seemed hopeful and trusting, with some sort of determination about it. Something that could not easily be put into words and indeed might never be. If Greta had mentioned such a thing he would have said, Don't be ridiculous. And she would have agreed with him, thinking that it was unnatural for people who saw each other daily, constantly, to have to go through explanations of any kind.

From: 'To Reach Japan', in Alice Munro, *Dear Life. Stories*, New York: Vintage Books 2013 (© 2012)

4 **marvel** wonder

a Try to identify who is who.

1 Peter: _____

2 Katy: _____

3 Greta: _____

b Describe in one sentence the situation the three characters are in. Predict in another sentence what you think the story will generally be about from the few hints given here.

_____
_____
_____

Narrative Prose – the Short Story

c 1 State what kind of narrator we have at the beginning of the passage.

___

2 Examine the text for indications of whose point of view the narrator takes. Highlight the indications in the passage and write the name of the character here:

___

d Re-write the paragraph from the point of view of Peter as a first-person narrator.

e State briefly what different effect is created by using a different point of view.

___
___
___
___

> **TIP**
> A first-person narrator can only talk about things he or she experiences, and can either provide feelings or hold them back.

3 Understanding microfiction

> OK. Should not have logged on to your email but suggest if going on marriedaffair.com don't use our children's names as password.
>
> From: www.guardian.co.uk/books/2012/oct/12/twitter-fiction-140-character-novels

The example of microfiction above was written by Helen Fielding, the author of *Bridget Jones's Diary*. Answer the following questions in brief notes.

1 Who is speaking? Who is being addressed?

___

2 What did each of the two people do?

___
___
___
___

3 What medium is the speaker using to communicate with the other person?

___

Helen Fielding

4 **CHALLENGE** Writing a short story

a The original microfiction in exercise **3** only hints at the background and possible consequences. Decide who the narrator is and write an introductory paragraph containing some information about the situation. Use phrases from the box below to help you.

> away on business • searching the internet for sth. • get bored • log on to his/her email • for the fun of it • flirtatious email from a stranger • online dating site • try out passwords • access sb's user account • our childrens' names • user profile • scandalous • disgusting behaviour

b Collect vocabulary that you could use in the main body of the story to develop the plot. You will need words/phrases from the wordfields 'relationships' and 'emotions'.

c Write your own short story (280–300 words) based on Helen Fielding's microfiction.

3 Living in the Global Village

Lead-in

1 Talking about globalization

Fill in the gaps with the correct preposition. In some cases more than one preposition is possible.

One feature which is typical _____ ¹ many varieties _____ ² economic globalization is that it involves companies using access _____ ³ cheap labour to achieve reductions _____ ⁴ costs. One common example _____ ⁵ this is manufacturing textiles _____ ⁶ Bangladesh. However, _____ ⁷ recent decades companies have also started to outsource services _____ ⁸ countries with lower wage costs: India and the Philippines, which have a large pool _____ ⁹ school-leavers educated _____ ¹⁰ English, are leading the way here. Apart _____ ¹¹ economic globalization, there are many instances _____ ¹² what could be called political or socio-cultural globalization, for example when consumers subscribe _____ ¹³ a satellite TV provider which allows them to watch programmes from all _____ ¹⁴ the world, or when reading people's reactions _____ ¹⁵ current events worldwide _____ ¹⁶ Twitter. However, even going _____ ¹⁷ holiday _____ ¹⁸ Mexico or visiting Australia _____ ¹⁹ a school exchange also contribute _____ ²⁰ increasing globalization.

▶ L19: Common collocations with prepositions, SB p. 182

2 Expanding vocabulary

a Fill in the blanks in the table below. All the words given are from the Lead-in.

Verb	Noun	Adjective
to affect		
to apply		
		cheap
	discussion	
	exchange	
to explain		
to fly		
to mix		
		safe
to subscribe		

b Now choose three of the words you have added to the table and write one sentence each on some aspect of globalization.

_____
_____
_____

Words in Context 3

Life in a global village

Look at 'Words in Context' (SB p. 62) again and fill in the empty boxes in the following wordlist.
In the 'Memory Support' box you can either …
- put the word or phrase in a sentence, or
- think of words belonging to the same family, or
- write down other collocations.

You can download this wordlist and edit it on your computer here:

Webcode
starwb-05

Word/Phrase	Memory support	German
(to) **overcome distances**	We can easily overcome distances with modern digital communication.	
	WORD FAMILY: technologist – technological – technologically	(die) moderne Technik, heutige Technologien
(to) **rely on** sb.	I'm relying on you to help me with this homework.	
(to) **connect virtually with** sb. ['vɜːtʃuəli]	Social networks enable us to connect virtually with people all over the world.	
(to) **spread news**		Nachrichten verbreiten
(to) **become interconnected**		verbunden/vernetzt werden
(to) **become increasingly interdependent**	Countries have become increasingly interdependent over the past century.	
a large multinational corporation	Large multinational corporations often have more power than some governments.	
(to) **outsource the production**	We outsource all our production to reduce costs.	
	WORD FAMILY: (to) develop – development – developer – developmental	ein Entwicklungsland
wages *(pl)*		Lohn, Gehalt
	WORD FAMILY: (to) consume – consumable – consumption – consumerism	(die) Verbraucher in den westlichen Industriestaaten

Living in the Global Village Chapter 3 31

3 Words in Context

Word/Phrase	Memory support	German
(to) **have an impact on** sth.		starken Einfluss auf etwas haben
	WORD FAMILY: forest – forestry – forester – forested – (to) deforest – (to) afforest – afforestation	Entwaldung, die Abholzung von Wäldern
water pollution	OTHER COLLOCATIONS: air/noise/light pollution – local/industrial pollution	
depletion of the ozone layer [dɪˈpliːʃn]		Abbau/Schädigung der Ozonschicht
	OTHER COLLOCATIONS: the global village/market – global player – global teamwork/solutions	die globale Erwärmung
	WORD FAMILY: climatic – climatology – climatologist – climatological	Klimawandel
	OTHER COLLOCATIONS: environmental pollution/impact/problem/influence – environmental issue/movement/group	Umweltschäden
an industrial country	OTHER COLLOCATIONS: industrial estate (BE) / industrial park (AE) – industrial relations/action	
global teamwork		globale Teamarbeit, weltweite Zusammenarbeit
	WORD FAMILY: (to) sustain – sustainable – sustainability	nachhaltig leben, ein nachhaltiges Leben führen
natural resources [rɪˈsɔːsɪz ☆ ˈriːsɔːsɪz] (pl)	The exploitation of natural resources is increasing rapidly in Brazil and Australia due to greater demand from China.	
international cooperation	We need much closer international cooperation if global warming is to be contained.	
a non-governmental organization (NGO)	NGOs are charities or other organizations which are completely independent of governments.	
(to) **agree on rules**	One of the biggest problems is how to agree on rules about how to combat climate change worldwide.	
	OTHER COLLOCATIONS: a common goal/idea/heritage	ein gemeinsames/allgemeines/häufiges Problem

Words in Context 3

3 What do you call …?   SB WiC ◀

Without looking at SB p. 62, give the answer to these questions.

What do you call …
1. … it when a company arranges for sb. outside the company to make things for the company? _____
2. … it when forests are cut down? _____
3. … people who buy goods or use services? _____
4. … large companies, which are often active worldwide? _____
5. … a regular amount of money that you earn, usually every week, in contrast to a salary earned every month? _____
6. … a large reduction in sth., e.g. the ozone layer, so that there is none or very little left? _____
7. … the process of making air or water dirty? _____
8. … when you need or depend on sb.? _____

4 Crossword   SB WiC ◀

a Use the clues to complete the crossword below. The words/phrases you need are all from 'Words in Context'.

1 involving the use of natural products and energy in a way that does not harm the planet

2 Digital communications … is one driving force behind globalization.

3/4 We need the planet's … … to live, but we have to protect them for future generations.

5/6 the harm we do to our surroundings

7 global … is one way to solve environmental problems

8 another word for 'working together'

9/10 parts of the world whose economies are not yet developed

11 The … nations, such as Russia and the USA, are responsible for a lot of air pollution.

12 Distance and time differences can be … in the 'global village'.

13/14 to link up with people using digital communication or the internet

15 being dependent on each other

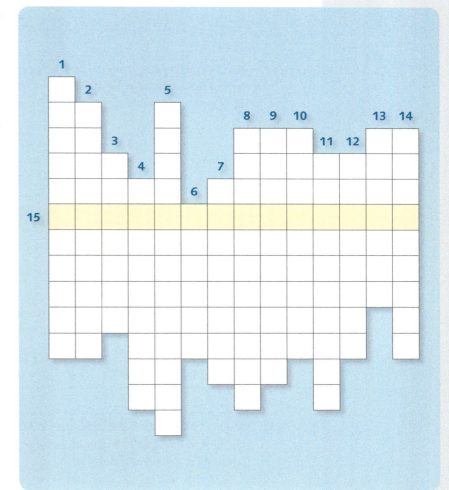

b Now write five sentences which include one of these words/phrases in each sentence.

Living in the Global Village — Chapter 3

3 Part A

Global citizens

FOCUS ON SKILLS MEDIATION

5 An exchange of views SB A1

Your father is interested in hearing more about the background of Tariq, your exchange partner from Mumbai. As Tariq does not speak any German and your father's English is rather rusty, you mediate between the two of them in English and German.

Father: Kannst du Tariq mal fragen, was seine Eltern beruflich machen?

You: Ja klar. Tariq, _____

Tariq: Well, my dad's an executive in a cotton mill. And my mum's got a part-time job at a call centre which belongs to a big UK bank.

You: _____

Father: Interessant. Hier hatten wir früher auch Baumwollfabriken, aber die meisten mussten wegen der Billigkonkurrenz aus Asien zumachen. Und die englischen Arbeiter sind bestimmt auch nicht über die indischen Call-Center glücklich. Was meint er dazu?

You: _____

Tariq: OK, it's not an easy subject, but the people in my father's factory have to work. Most of them are very poor, compared to Europeans. And he shouldn't forget that in the early 20th century it was British cotton mills which destroyed the Indian textile industry.

You: _____

Father: Gut, aber seine Mutter muss doch nicht arbeiten, oder? Als Manager verdient man auch in Indien ganz gut.

You: _____

Tariq: Yes, he's right. She doesn't have to go out to work. But we're saving up for a new house, and Mum wants to help out. She's independent and likes to get out of the house.

You: _____

Tariq: Mum and Dad aren't the only ones involved in globalization. My older sister Sarita is the best in her class at maths and she gives private tuition in maths on the internet to students in Britain and Belgium.

You: _____

▶ S21: Mediation of written and oral texts, WB pp. 81–83

Chapter 3 Living in the Global Village

Global citizens 3

Father: Vielleicht könnte sie deiner Schwester helfen. Sie ist schlecht in Mathe, aber gut in Englisch. Frage, was es kostet. Es darf nicht zu viel kosten.

You: _____

_____

_____

Tariq: Five euros an hour.

You: _____

Father: Fünf Euro die Stunde! Das ist ja spottbillig. Wir zahlen sonst 20!

You: _____

Tariq: But I thought you were against globalization …

6 Listening comprehension

SB A3

In April 2013, 1129 people died and 2515 were injured in Bangladesh when a building containing a garment factory collapsed due to poor safety standards. This highlighted the problems involved in Western firms outsourcing production to low-cost countries. Listen to the editorial panel of the Canadian *Toronto Star* discussing the issue and answer the questions.

1 Why is the garment industry important for Bangladesh?

It accounts for …
a ☐ 10% of its total economy.
b ☐ 20% of Bangladesh's economy.
c ☐ 50% of the economy.

2 What figures are mentioned for the countries where Bangladeshi exports go to? (Draw lines to connect the countries and figures concerned.)

Canada	
the USA	60%
the EU	4%–5%

3 What has Joe Fresh done to help the victims' families and improve conditions? (More than one answer is correct.)

The company is …
a ☐ building a new factory with better safety standards.
b ☐ providing jobs for other family members.
c ☐ giving compensation for the victims' families.
d ☐ sending auditors to work out new corporate standards.

4 What does Andrew think should be done about the situation?

He takes the view that …
a ☐ workers will be poorly paid if we want cheap clothes.
b ☐ in future we'll just have to pay through the nose so that workers are better paid.
c ☐ working conditions can be improved without wrecking the Bangladeshi economy.

5 How much are workers paid per month in Bangladesh?

a ☐ $38   b ☐ $138   c ☐ $183

6 How have working conditions in the country been developing?

They have been …
a ☐ getting worse.
b ☐ getting better.
c ☐ remaining stable.

You can download the audio file and transcript here:

Webcode starwb-06

▶ S1: Listening for information, WB pp. 56–57
▶ S22: Making and taking notes, WB p. 84

Living in the Global Village — Chapter 3

3 Part A

FOCUS ON LANGUAGE VOCABULARY AND STYLE

7 Did you get that? — SB A4

One of the most frequently used words in spoken English is *get*. In formal written English, however, it is usually bad style to use it. Imagine that you are working for a British organization investigating the effects of a consumer boycott of Chinese goods (see also SB A5).
The text below is part of a formal report. Cross out *get* or the *get* phrases and replace them with a better alternative. The words in the box below will help you.

| arrive at • become • be given • be told • catch • have to • meet • receive • understand |

We got to hear _____ ¹ about the factory closing at Shilong New Town when we were in Beijing. When we got to _____ ² the factory, nobody local was prepared to explain why the condenser dryer factory there had closed until we got to know _____ ³ Lu, who had worked there as a security guard. At first it was difficult to get _____ ⁴ what he was saying – he spoke fast and with a strong Sichuan accent. He said he had got _____ ⁵ the job six months before after getting _____ ⁶ news that there was a vacancy. Initially, everything went well, but after a few months he realized that the situation was changing. There were rumours of workers being laid off, and his bosses had got _____ ⁷ nervous and edgy. He said he'd got to _____ ⁸ be careful, because there were informers everywhere, and he didn't want the police to get _____ ⁹ him. They were not happy about Chinese workers talking to foreigners.

▶ L18: Using the exact word, SB p. 182

8 Nations and nationalities — SB A4

Complete the following statements.

1 Our next-door neighbours are from Helsinki. They're _____.

2 My English teacher's from Glasgow, so she's _____.

3 Hyundai isn't Japanese. It's _____.

4 When I was last in Dublin, several _____ told me they hated 'Irish jokes' because they make _____ look stupid.

5 In London we went to Soho and saw a lot of _____ restaurants with names like 'Crispy Duck', 'Little Wu' or 'Loon Tau'. Usually there are also quite a few _____ eating inside, which is always a good sign.

6 Last year in Amsterdam we noticed that most _____ seemed to speak both English and German.

7 I met quite a few _____ while I was in New Zealand. One was from Cardiff, two were from Bristol, and one was from Aberdeen.

8 My next-door neighbours are _____. They're from Warsaw.

> **TIP**
>
> Most nationality nouns have regular plurals, e.g. *Canadians, Malaysians*. However, nouns ending in *-ese*, e.g. *Japanese, Vietnamese*, do not add *-s*. Words like *British, Dutch, English, French, Irish* and *Welsh* can be used as adjectives, e.g. *Rhiannon is **Welsh***. To form a noun phrase you need to either use *the* followed by the adjective, e.g. ***The Irish** usually celebrate St Patrick's Day*, or you add *people* after the adjective, e.g. *Most **English people** I know prefer coffee to tea.*

36 Chapter 3 Living in the Global Village

Global citizens 3

9 A slang quiz   SB A4

The sentences below contain US slang expressions (underlined), many of which are also used in British English. Choose the correct equivalent in neutral language from the alternatives given.

1. He earns a hundred <u>grand</u> before taxes.
   - a ☐ dollars
   - b ☐ million dollars
   - c ☐ thousand

2. They went out to the pub on Friday night and <u>got plastered</u>.
   - a ☐ got drunk
   - b ☐ got injured
   - c ☐ went crazy

3. This is a sale, so everything is <u>up for grabs</u>.
   - a ☐ cheap
   - b ☐ slightly damaged
   - c ☐ available for purchase

4. OK, I get the message. You don't need to <u>blow a fuse</u>.
   - a ☐ get somebody else to do the job
   - b ☐ get angry, lose your temper
   - c ☐ hit me

5. The new movie was <u>a bomb</u>.
   - a ☐ fantastic
   - b ☐ violent
   - c ☐ awful

6. This job is <u>pure gravy</u>.
   - a ☐ easy money
   - b ☐ very well paid
   - c ☐ really difficult

7. Let's go to a restaurant and <u>pig out</u>.
   - a ☐ enjoy ourselves
   - b ☐ eat a lot, overeat
   - c ☐ spend lots of money on food.

8. I think we need to <u>hang tough on our decision</u>.
   - a ☐ stick with what we decided
   - b ☐ modify our demands
   - c ☐ toughen up our demands

> **TIP**
>
> Slang is informal vocabulary which can usually only be understood by people from a particular social group. Its main function is to show that people belong to a specific group, i.e. to mark them out as different from other groups. Examples are teenage slang, army slang.

10 CHALLENGE Informal to formal   SB A4

Change the informal dialogue below into a formal email complaining about the hotel described in the conversation. First underline the informal expressions in the dialogue. (You may have to check words in a dictionary.) Then write a formal email, replacing the informal expressions by more formal ones. The words in the vocabulary box will help you.

> charge £100 per night • complain to sb. • eventually • facilities • lose your temper • my girlfriend and myself • not fresh • not the standard I would expect • refund sth. in full • ruin the weekend • shout and scream abuse at sb. • what is more

Chris: How was your weekend in Hastings with Jane? Was the hotel any good?

Mike: No, it was awful! And it cost us a packet, as well – 200 quid for two nights.

Chris: Wow, that's steep.

Mike: Not only that. It was a grotty place. The furniture looked about 30 years old, and the bathroom fittings were dodgy. In the shower you couldn't adjust the water temperature, so at first you got freezing cold water and then, when the warm water came on, it was so hot you couldn't stand it. The cooked breakfast was a disaster. It was cold by the time we got it, and the fried tomatoes and mushrooms were out of a tin.

Chris: Didn't you complain?

Mike: Of course. After breakfast on Saturday morning I went to the reception and told them politely about the bathroom and the cold breakfast. The mattress felt like it was as old as the furniture, so we didn't get much kip, either. The receptionist started to get stroppy, so I asked to see the manager. He wasn't available, she said. I should try again later. When I tried again in the afternoon, he still wasn't there. The next morning I managed to get him. When I listed all the things wrong with the hotel and asked for my money back he went bananas and started shouting and screaming. What a prat!

Chris: So what are you going to do?

Mike: I'm going to write an email to the general manager of the hotel chain complaining about the standards at the hotel. It's the Blue Star Hotel in Chalfont Road. Whatever you do, avoid it like the plague.

▶ S15: Writing a formal letter or email, WB p. 74

▶ S25: Using a dictionary, WB pp. 86–89

▶ L14: Formal and informal English, SB p. 178

3 Part A

11 Working at a factory   SB A5

a Collect vocabulary from the wordfield 'factory' in the mindmap which has been begun for you below.

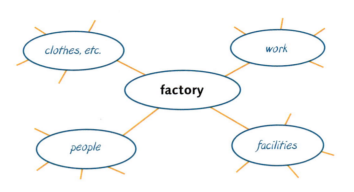

b Imagine you are a worker or boss at the factory described in SB **A5** (p. 66). Write a diary entry (70–130 words) about the lock-out, using words you have collected in your mindmap.

_____
_____
_____
_____
_____
_____
_____
_____

12 Which past?   SB A5

In the text below, put the verbs in brackets in the simple past or past perfect. If both can be used, give both. Put any adverbs in the correct position.

After I ___(had) finished___ (finish) school, I _____ ¹ (start) work at a factory.

I _____ ² (already/have) some experience of factory work in the school

holidays, because I _____ ³ (work) as a labourer in various places since I

_____ ⁴ (be) sixteen. Before I _____ ⁵ (apply) for the job I

_____ ⁶ (talk) to a few friends about the company that _____ ⁷ (run)

the factory. Most of them _____ ⁸ (say) that it _____ ⁹ (be) well

run, but one of them _____ ¹⁰ (disagree), saying that he _____ ¹¹

(be) sure they _____ ¹² (exploit) their workers. I _____ ¹³

(remember) what he _____ ¹⁴ (tell) us several months later, when we

_____ ¹⁵ (suddenly/be locked) out by the management.

Chapter 3   Living in the Global Village

Part B   3

Looking after the global village

13 Word quiz   SB B2 ◀

Use your dictionary to find out more about the following words from text **B2** in the SB (pp. 72–73).

a What is the difference between the following words: *garbage – junk, craft – vessel*?

garbage: _____

junk: _____

craft: _____

vessel: _____

b How is a *boat* usually different from a *ship*?

_____

c Which pronunciation is correct? Underline the correct one.

1 cruise: a [kruːz]   b [kruːɪz]   c [kruːɪs]

2 knots: a [knɒts]   b [nəʊts]   c [nɒts]

d The following words are pronounced differently in American English (AE) and British English (BE). Note that in each case one of the pronunciations is wrong. Label each pronunciation as *AE*, *BE* or *wrong*.

1 raft: a [ræft] _____   b [reft] _____   c [rɑːft] _____

2 mast: a [mæst] _____   b [meɪst] _____   c [mɑːst] _____

3 debris: a ['debrɪs] _____   b ['debriː] _____   c [də'briː] _____

4 fiancée: a [fi'ɒnseɪ] _____   b ['faɪənsi] _____   c [ˌfiːɑːn'seɪ] _____

▶ S25: Using a dictionary, WB pp. 86–89

14 An interview with Roz   SB B2 ◀

Complete the interview with Roz Savage by writing what she might have said.
You can use the vocabulary in the box to help you if you wish.

> amazed • fantastic idea • hundreds of miles • make people aware • mast • not seen a soul •
> plane's cockpit • pollute • really weird • thousands of plastic bottles

Interviewer: What was your reaction when you saw 'Junk' in the middle of nowhere?

Roz: *Well,* _____

_____

Interviewer: Can you describe it to us?

Roz: *Yes, of course.* _____

_____

Interviewer: What were they doing out in the Pacific on a junk raft?

Roz: _____

_____

Living in the Global Village   Chapter 3

3 Part B

FOCUS ON SKILLS — WRITING
Writing paragraphs

15 More about global warming SB B3

> This means that the Earth's heat is held inside the atmosphere, raising the planet's average temperature. The warming effect has been intensifying recently, due to the emissions caused by cars, planes, factories and power stations, which could have disastrous consequences for us all.

1 Decide which of the three sentences would form the best topic sentence for the first paragraph on the left. (Tick the correct box.)

a ☐ Many experts have warned about the possibility of global warming.
b ☐ Global warming is caused by a complicated process called the greenhouse effect.
c ☐ There can be no doubt that global warming is increasing.

> This runaway greenhouse effect would push temperatures up so high that trees and crops across the world would die, which in turn would accelerate the pace of global warming, leading to an exponential rise in temperature.

2 Now supply a suitable topic sentence for the second paragraph.

_____
_____
_____

3 Read the topic sentence of the third paragraph and use the notes below to supply the supporting sentences.

Gulf Stream • currently guarantee • Europe • a milder climate

> On the other hand, other scientists warn that the melting ice coming from the North and South Poles could affect the Gulf Stream.

_____
_____
_____

change in flow • Gulf Stream → Arctic conditions • Europe

_____
_____

4 Finally, write a concluding sentence for the third paragraph which summarizes its ideas.

▶ S13: The stages of writing, WB pp. 72–73

_____
_____

16 Where's the apostrophe? SB B4

Underline the correct alternative in the following sentences.

1 The amount of CFCs peaked at the earths/earth's/earths' surface 10 years ago.
2 The United States/State's/States' lead was followed by the majority of countries.
3 If CFC use had continued, todays/today's/todays' hole would be much larger.
4 People talked about it over the neighbours/neighbour's/neighbours' fence.
5 The Montreal Protocols/Protocol's/Protocols' success was a pleasant surprise.
6 Peoples/People's/Peoples' attitudes have changed.
7 The United Nations/Nation's/Nations' support has been invaluable.
8 Sara Lajeunesse/Lajeunesse'/Lajeunesse's article outlines the development.
9 The boss/boss'/boss's car stopped at the gate.

Chapter 3   Living in the Global Village

Focus on Literature

Poetry

▶ S9: Reading and analysing poetry, WB pp. 66–68

1 'Pictures made out of words' SB A ◀

Match the following images to a suitable abstract noun from the list on the right. There may be more than one connotation for some of them.

1 a wilted rose _____
2 sitting on the sofa with a cat on your lap _____
3 a child handing her favourite doll to another _____
4 tears in sb's eyes _____
5 an embrace _____
6 a person screaming abuse at another _____
7 getting a long-awaited phone call _____
8 a shotgun aimed at a person _____
9 weeping at a graveside _____
10 curled up in an easy chair watching the flames in the fireplace _____
11 a flower losing its petals _____
12 two people kissing _____
13 falling onto a soft chair _____
14 someone stamping their foot _____
15 tearing up a piece of paper after writing on it _____
16 two hands entwined _____

hate

frustration

love

contentment

loss

relief

2 Who is the speaker of the poem? SB B1 ◀

a Read the following poem and while you read, make notes in the on who you think is speaking, and who is being addressed by the speaker.

> **My Life in the Garden** *by Roger McGough*
>
> It is a lovely morning, what with the sun, etc.
> And I won't hear a word said against it.
>
> Standing in the garden I have no idea of the time
> Even though I am wearing the sundial hat you gave me.
>
> 5 What the scene requires is an aural dimension
> And, chuffed to high heaven, birds provide it.
>
> I think about my life in the garden
> About what has gone before
>
> And about what is yet to come.
>
> 10 And were my feet not set in concrete,
> I would surely jump for joy.
>
> From: Roger McGough, *Everyday Eclipses*, London: Penguin, 2003 © 2002

> **TIP**
> In poems with a first-person perspective it seems clear at first sight whose perspective it is – but look carefully, because it is usually not the poet that is speaking.

4 **sundial** *Sonnenuhr*
5 **aural** to do with hearing
6 **chuffed to high heaven** extremely happy

41

Focus on Literature

Poetry

b Note down who is speaking, who they are speaking to, and how this becomes completely clear only at the end of the poem.

c Go through the poem again and highlight the phrases or whole lines that contain hints at the identity of the speaker. Think about the effect of the last lines on your appreciation of the whole poem. Choose words from the list below that best characterize your feelings about the poem, and write a short statement.

> amused • annoyed • irritated • disappointed • puzzled • satisfied • surprised

3 Sound devices

Sometimes children use poetry when playing, e.g. when counting out to see who is next in turn for whatever game they are playing. Read the following so-called counting-out rhyme out loud to yourself:

> Hinx, minx, the old witch winks,
>   The fat begins to fry
> Nobody at home but jumping Joan,
>   Father, mother and I.
> 5 Stick, stock, stone dead,
>   Blind man can't see;
> Every knave will have a slave,
>   You or I must be HE.
>
> From: *I Saw Esau. The Schoolchild's Pocket Book*, ed. Iona & Peter Opie, London 1992

7 **knave** (old use) dishonest man or boy

a Mark the sound devices (see SB p. 81), using different colours for different devices.

b Explain briefly why this type of poem relies so heavily on sound devices.

c Compare the effect(s) of the sound devices used here with those used in the poem you chose when studying part B of the Poetry module (SB pp. 81–82) and state what is different and how the effects differ.

Going Places 4

Lead-in

1 What does it mean   SB L-i ◀

Choose the correct explanation for the concepts underlined below.

1 <u>Multitasking</u> is when you …
   a ☐ work for a multinational company.
   b ☐ speak many different languages.
   c ☐ can do several different things at the same time.

2 An <u>aptitude</u> is …
   a ☐ a natural ability or skill at doing sth.
   b ☐ something you use on your smartphone.
   c ☐ a tendency to do sth.

3 <u>Attention</u> means …
   a ☐ making a student stay in after school as punishment.
   b ☐ the act of attending an event.
   c ☐ the act of listening to, looking at or thinking about sth.

4 By <u>cognitive impairment</u> we mean …
   a ☐ being able to use both sides of the brain.
   b ☐ damage to the thinking process.
   c ☐ the ability to recognize shapes.

5 A <u>salary uplift</u> refers to …
   a ☐ a pay rise.
   b ☐ an expensive cosmetic operation.
   c ☐ an increase in the tax paid on salaries.

6 <u>Overall intelligence</u> means …
   a ☐ a group of skilled blue-collar workers.
   b ☐ general, not specific, intelligence.
   c ☐ intelligence found everywhere.

7 <u>Dating agencies</u> are agencies which …
   a ☐ help business people to fix appointments.
   b ☐ assist organizations in storing data.
   c ☐ organize meetings between people who are looking for a partner.

8 To <u>outperform</u> is to …
   a ☐ do more theatre or other performances than another person.
   b ☐ achieve better results than sb./sth. else.
   c ☐ do street theatre, i.e. theatre outside.

2 Alternatives   SB L-i ◀

What other ways of expressing the ideas below can you find on SB p. 87?

1 There is an annual increase of 12% in the number of international students.

2 Sixty-three per cent of the people in the survey have dated somebody speaking a different language.

3 More than one third of businesses specifically want people because of their language skills.

> ■ TIP
> Notice that in English we usually put the past participle after the noun: *those **surveyed**, the people **interviewed**, the passage **mentioned**.*
> Contrast this with German: *die **befragten** Personen, die **erwähnte** Passage.*

▶ S28: Working with charts and graphs, WB p. 91

4 Words in Context

The importance of speaking languages

You can download this wordlist and edit it on your computer here:

Webcode
starwb-07

Look at 'Words in Context' (SB p. 88) again and fill in the empty boxes in the following wordlist. In the 'Memory Support' box you can either…
- put the word or phrase in a sentence, or
- think of words belonging to the same family, or
- write down other collocations.

Word/Phrase	Memory support	German
a foreign language ['fɒrɪn]	I love the kick of going to foreign countries, seeing different things and speaking foreign languages.	
essential		unabdingbar
a lingua franca ['lɪŋgwə 'fræŋkə]	Because of the many different local languages, Swahili and English are important lingua francas in East Africa.	
	OTHER COLLOCATIONS: a native speaker	eine Mutter-/Heimatsprache
(to) advance your English [əd'vɑːns ☆ əd'væns]	OTHER COLLOCATIONS: (to) advance your career/your knowledge/ the cause of democracy	
intercultural skills	In the days of globalization, intercultural skills are just as important as good qualifications.	
	We often go on holiday abroad.	im Ausland, ins Ausland
a school exchange [ɪks'tʃeɪndʒ]	OTHER COLLOCATIONS:	Ein Schüleraustausch
a host country [həʊst ☆ hoʊst]	OTHER COLLOCATIONS:	ein Gastland (host = Gastgeber)
	OTHER COLLOCATIONS: (to) gain confidence/strength/access/entry	Erfahrungen über eine andere Kultur sammeln/gewinnen
(to) develop an awareness of different nations	School exchanges help pupils to develop an awareness of different nations.	

Words in Context 4

Word/Phrase	Memory support	German
(to) **contribute to** sth.	WORD FAMILY:	zu etw. beitragen
	OTHER COLLOCATIONS: mutual admiration/respect/support – mutual dislike/distrust	gegenseitige internationale Verständigung
a vital opportunity ['vaɪtl]	You shouldn't miss this vital opportunity to study abroad.	
(to) **broaden your horizons**		den eigenen Horizont erweitern
(to) **accommodate** sb.	This hotel can accommodate up to 500 guests.	
a range of activities		eine Reihe/Vielzahl von Aktivitäten
(to) **be given the opportunity to do** sth.		die Chance bekommen, etwas zu tun
volunteering	WORD FAMILY:	ehrenamtliche Arbeit, Freiwilligendienst
(to) **meet new challenges**	She decided it was time to meet new challenges and find herself a new job.	
	WORD FAMILY: life-enhancing – life-giving – life-saving – life-threatening	eine lebensverändernde/ unvergessliche Erfahrung
(to) **boost** sb.'s **self-confidence**	Coping successfully with difficulties will boost your self-confidence.	
(to) **last a lifetime**	If you want friendships to last a lifetime, you have to keep in contact.	

4 Words in Context

3 Collocations in context SB WiC ◀

Match the two halves of the sentences and highlight the phrases from 'Words in Context'.

1 For my dream job I need to gain …
2 They say travel broadens …
3 I've decided it's time to meet a …
4 I think studying abroad is a vital …
5 School exchanges contribute to mutual …
6 If he gets this job, it'll really boost …
7 My dad says the best way to advance …
8 Lauren has excellent intercultural …

a international understanding.
b my English is to study in London for a year.
c skills – she has worked abroad for 5 years.
d his self-confidence.
e experience in computer languages.
f opportunity if you want to work in international marketing.
g new challenge and start learning Chinese.
h your horizons.

1 _____ 2 _____ 3 _____ 4 _____ 5 _____ 6 _____ 7 _____ 8 _____

4 Changing word classes SB WiC ◀

Complete the sentences using words from the box on the left. They are all in the 'Words in Context' list, but are used in a different word class here. A noun, adjective or verb in the list may be a verb or noun in this exercise. Write *verb* or *noun* in the space provided.

- advance •
- challenge •
- essential •
- exchange •
- host • range •
- volunteer

1 The rebels and the government agreed to _____ prisoners. ☐

2 Leonard has _____ me to a game of chess. ☐

3 We see this as a major _____ in medical science. ☐

4 One of the _____ of language learning is knowing the grammar. ☐

5 We want to go to Chennai as _____, to help the poor. ☐

6 We don't know yet which country will _____ the Olympic Games. ☐

7 Average temperatures in Los Angeles _____ from around 13°C in winter to 21°C in summer. ☐

5 Jumbled words SB WiC ◀

Unscramble the underlined words below, which are all taken from 'Words in Context'.

1 Jim was our tosh for the evening at the restaurant. _____

2 It's vailt to have a good dictionary when you learn a language. _____

3 Our school wants to tobos interest in spending a year abroad. _____

4 I find that going abroad definitely helps me to doreban ym rhosinoz. _____ _____

5 I'm not sure that the hotel can dommacatcoe so many guests during the summer. _____

6 Don't you agree that ofringe food always seems so much more exciting? _____

7 There is an increasing seranewas that intercultural skills are important in business. _____

8 During her year abroad, Kylie's fels-dinoccefen increased enormously. _____

Chapter 4 Going Places

Part A

In a foreign classroom

6 Peter's errors
SB A2

Peter's English (see SB **A2**, Partner B, p. 118) is now pretty good, but he still makes some mistakes. Underline the correct forms in his sentences below.

1 Hi, I am a German exchange student in the USA / who is in the USA / who has been in the USA since August 2014.
2 I stay with a host family, who / I stay with a host family which / I'm staying with a host family who took the responsibility to take care of me for a year / of looking after me for a year / to look after me since a year.
3 During the week I go to high school, where I have a lot of interesting classes / I'm going to the high school, where I'm having a lot of interesting classes / I go to the high school where I have a lot of interesting classes.
4 I try getting to the point where you guys can't hear my accent anymore. / I'm trying getting to the point where you guys can't hear my accent anymore. / I'm trying to get to the point where you guys can't hear my accent anymore.
5 I have already learned many other things since I got here. / I already learned many other things since I've got here. / I'm already learning many other things since I'm here.
6 It's about the best thing that ever happen to me / ever could have happen to me / could have ever happened to me.
7 I learned about customs, morals, beliefs, the little different food / the slightly different food / the bit different food, and lots of other things.
8 I now understand radio and TV shows in the other language / in a other language / in a different language.
9 I make friends and contribute tightening our cultural bonds / toward tightening our cultural bonds / to tighten our cultural bonds.
10 I discovered all the little differences, like in street signs, my views and everything I took for granted is suddenly just upside down / and my views and all I took for granted suddenly is just upside down / and my views and everything I took for granted are suddenly just upside down.
11 I really got open-minded. / I've become really open-minded. / I really became open-minded.

7 At a US high school
SB A2

In the recording, you will hear two students who spent a year at a US high school talk about their impressions. Sofiya is from the Ukraine, Zarrina from the Asian republic of Tajikistan. Both countries used to be part of the former Soviet Union.

a Listening for gist: Listen once and tick the correct boxes.
1 On the whole, what were their impressions of the USA?
   a ☐ positive
   b ☐ negative
   c ☐ neutral

2 What aspects of the USA do they like? (More than one answer is correct.)
   a ☐ sport
   b ☐ school
   c ☐ the environment
   d ☐ Americans' attitude to their society
   e ☐ the natural landscape
   f ☐ the cities
   g ☐ TV

TIP

After a year in the USA, both girls speak English well. However, they do still have an accent. One aspect which can easily lead to misunderstandings is the way they pronounce words like *live, hit* as if they were *leave, heat*. One of the girls sometimes mumbles or speaks very fast. On the other hand, their English in this extract is fairly simple. You will probably need to listen at least twice to answer all the questions.

You can download the audio file and transcript here:

Webcode starwb-08

▶ S1: Listening for information, WB pp. 56–57

4 Part A

You can download the audio file and transcript here:

Webcode
starwb-08

b **Listening for detail:** Listen again and tick the correct boxes.

1 How old are the two girls?
   a ☐ Zarrina is 17, Sofiya 18.
   b ☐ Zarrina is 18, Sofiya 17.
   c ☐ They are both the same age: 17.

2 Sofiya says that the US is …
   a ☐ just like in the movies.
   b ☐ not like in the movies.
   c ☐ a bit like in the movies

3 Zarrina says that …
   (More than one answer is possible.)
   a ☐ in Tajikistan they do a lot of maths and have more homework than in the USA.
   b ☐ in the USA they have more homework.
   c ☐ they do more sport in the USA.
   d ☐ in Tajikistan they teach you to think more critically.
   e ☐ they teach you to think more critically in the USA.
   f ☐ in Tajikistan you memorize things a lot; you don't analyse or share your thoughts and ideas.

4 Sofiya thinks that teachers in the USA …
   a ☐ aren't as friendly as in Ukraine.
   b ☐ are kinder than back home.
   c ☐ are not as good as back home.
   d ☐ teach sport better than in Ukraine.

5 Before she came to the USA, she thought that Americans were …
   a ☐ very clever, but now she's not so sure.
   b ☐ more environmentally friendly than Ukrainians.
   c ☐ pretty stupid, but now she's seen so many smart kids in the USA.
   d ☐ obsessed with guns.

6 Now her impression is that Americans …
   a ☐ want to know what's going on in the country.
   b ☐ don't read newspapers.
   c ☐ are obsessed with crime.
   d ☐ watch TV too much.

7 What, in Sofiya's view, are the problems with eating in America?
   (More than one answer is possible.)
   a ☐ There are too many sweets, which is very tempting.
   b ☐ There are too many treats, like hamburgers and peanut butter.
   c ☐ A lot of the food is bad for the environment.
   d ☐ The portions of food are huge.
   e ☐ Many people eat too fast.

8 What are their favourite foods in the USA? (Complete the sentences.)

   a Zarrina likes _____.

   b Sofiya likes _____.

9 What impact has the stay in the USA had on Zarrina's English?

_____

_____

_____

▶ S1: Listening for information, WB pp. 56–57

In a foreign classroom

8 I wouldn't have missed it for the world!
SB A2

Fill in the missing words, which are all from the two A2 texts in the SB. The number of spaces corresponds to the number of letters missing.

I've been s_____ in Melbourne now for three months. My h___ f_____ consists of a h___ b_____, who is my official e_____ p_____, a h___ s_____ and of course two h___ p_____. I'm really enjoying my s___ here in Oz, and I'm so glad I chose it for my e_____ t___. I came here to r_____ my English l_____ s_____ which seems to have worked, because I'm now much more f_____ in the language than I was in the school c_____ back home. I tend to p___ u_ a lot of c_____ p_____ from my schoolmates, but I also learn u_____ w____ by reading the paper and watching TV.

By now I think I've got over my c_____ s_____, and I'm beginning to feel at home in Australian c_____. To be honest, before I came here I was u_____ of how German I really am. You only notice that when you come across people from another culture who were r_____ w____ d_____ i_____ from those you grew up with. I now feel a lot more o___-m_____ than when I first arrived here. It's been a real privilege to e_____ e_____ l___ down under. I wouldn't have missed it for the world!

9 CHALLENGE Thinking about everyday life in Germany
SB A2

What did Emma (see SB A2, Partner A, p.91) find unusual about German everyday life, both at school and outside school? Choose two things she mentions from each area which most surprised you. Describe them and say why you find them surprising.

> become aware of sth. • be struck by sth. • notice sth. • realize sth. • what was striking

▶ S13: The stages of writing, WB pp. 72–73

4 Part A

10 Writing an informal email SB A2

Your Irish penfriend has heard that her school is organizing a two-week exchange with a German school. Reply to her email, telling her what you think. The vocabulary in the box will help you.

> Hi
> I've just had some fantastic news. Our school is setting up a two-week exchange next April with a school near Kassel. I'm really keen, but I'm worried about the cost. People say Germany's very expensive, and my dad's out of work. And anyway, two weeks isn't very long, and I don't think it'll help my German that much. What do you think?
> All the best
> Roisin

> agree with you • awesome • brilliant • careful with your money • depend on • don't get too excited • even in two weeks • fantastic • go for it • go on an exchange • great to hear from you • it'll get much better • pay for sth. • pocket money • there may be other problems • two weeks is too short • your family's … comes first

▶ S14: Creative writing, WB pp. 73–74
▶ S15: Writing a formal letter or email, WB p. 74

_____
_____
_____
_____
_____
_____

FOCUS ON SKILLS VIEWING

11 Film techniques quiz SB A3

Test your knowledge of film techniques by labelling the following pictures with the correct type of camera 'shot'.

1 _____

2 _____

3 _____

4 _____

5 _____

6 _____

▶ S2: Viewing a film, SB pp. 121–122

In a foreign classroom

FOCUS ON SKILLS READING
Reading effectively

12 What's in it for me? SB A6

Look at the text on SB p. 97 again. The focus this time is on how the European Day of Languages could help you. Answer the questions below.

1 Scan the text to find the following words. Say where they are in the text and explain why they are used in the text.

   workout: line _____   brain power: line _____

   _____
   _____
   _____

> **TIP**
> When referring to the contents of a text, the following phrases are helpful:
> - The text says/states/points out that …
> - In the text it says/explains that …
> - It says in the text that this …
>
> Do **not** write: ~~It is said in the text that …~~ or ~~In the text stands that …~~
> These are literal translations from German and are never used.

2 Now skim the text to find out how, according to the text, knowing other foreign languages would give you an advantage when applying for jobs. Then explain why in your own words.

   _____
   _____
   _____
   _____

▶ S4: Skimming and scanning, SB pp. 123–124

3 Take an in-depth look at lines 8–12 of the text and explain, in your own words, what the word *jubilant* means and why the organizers chose to make the Day 'jubilant'.

   _____
   _____
   _____
   _____

13 A hard language? SB A7

a Correct these typical errors made by Germans learning English. State which field they are from – *grammar*, *prepositions*, *spelling* or *vocabulary* – in the space provided.

1 I'm making my exams next week. _____
2 I don't like to work to much. _____
3 Our holiday cottage is at the coast. _____
4 I speak English fairly good. _____
5 I've seen him in town yesterday. _____
6 This attitude is typical for him. _____
7 I said him that I couldn't come. _____
8 I can't find her adress. _____

b **CHALLENGE** What do you think about the poem on SB p. 98? Explain your opinion. You may find the words in the vocabulary box useful for this.

> amusing • confusing • fascinating • funny • intelligent • interesting • irregular forms • misleading • nonsense words • playing with language • silly • strange

Going Places   Chapter 4

4 Part B

Work and life experience

14 Describing and generalizing SB B1 ◀

Use the vocabulary in the box to describe what is happening in the photos shown below.
Then make generalizations about what normally happens at summer camps.

> give assistance to sb. in doing sth. • help sb. to do sth. • include sth. • in photo 1 / the first photo
> we/you (can) see • in other words • involve doing sth. • make things • supervise sb. •
> take part in sth. • teach sb. to do sth. • the older person • the picture shows

TIP 1
Use the progressive form to describe what is happening in photos or stills from a video. If you are unsure exactly what is going on, you can use phrases like *it looks like he's doing …* or *he seems/appears to be …-ing*.
Use the simple form to make generalizations about what people do, e.g. *At summer camp people learn things like …*

TIP 2
Don't use the definite article to talk in general about the way students live at a summer camp: *One of the attractions* **of life in the camp** *…* or *What I would like* **about camp life** *is …* . In German it would be *des Lebens im Lager* and *über das Lagerleben*.

Giving examples
There are various phrases to introduce examples: *for example …*, *for instance …*, *such as …* and (informally) *like …* . Be careful with the abbreviation *e.g.* It is only used before the example given and after a reference to the class of things of which an example is given: *Some summer camps, e.g. those in the western United States, also offer courses in mountaineering.*

▶ L2: Simple present and present progressive, SB pp. 165–166

Work and life experience 4

15 CHALLENGE Summer camp in Germany SB B2

Chris, your Scottish partner on last year's school exchange, wants to find a summer camp in Germany where he can learn to windsurf and sail. He's in his second year of learning German at Hamilton Academy, Aberdeen, and would like to improve his German at the same time, but is a bit worried that his German won't be good enough.

You've found an international summer camp, *Feriencamp Wellenreiter*, which you think is just right for him. Read their website and write him an email giving him the details.

He needs to know the following:
- Where is it, what age group is it for and what does it offer?
- How long are the courses and what do they cost?
- Other activities
- Accommodation (how many beds to a room?)
- Food and drink
- Language support (do instructors speak English?)
- The organization's contact details

▶ S21: Mediation of written and oral texts, WB pp. 81–83

---

www.wellenreiter-feriencamp.de/home/

Windsurf- und Segelschule • Feriencamp

WELLENREITER

Ferienkurse

für Jugendliche im Alter von 15 bis 17 Jahren – alles inklusive.
- 7 Nächte (Einführungskurs) / 14 Nächte (Aufbaukurs)
- Volle Verpflegung
- vielseitiges Wassersportprogramm
- Betreuung durch geschulte, professionelle WassersportlehrerInnen
- Hauseigener Sandstrand an der Kieler Bucht
- zusätzliche Aktivitäten: Beachvolleyball, Angeltouren, Bananaboats, Wakeboard, Paddeln mit Kajaks und Kanus
- nur 50 Min. vom Kieler Hauptbahnhof

Mahlzeiten

8.30 – 9.30 reichhaltiges Frühstücksbüffet
12.30 – 13.30 „kleine" warme Mahlzeit zum Krafttanken: z.B. Hot Dog, Hamburger, Spaghetti
18.30 – 19.30 warmes Abendessen, z.B. Schnitzel, Frikadellen, jeweils mit Gemüse und Salat, oder Grillabend mit Wurst, Fleisch und Salaten. Obst, Mineralwasser und Saft stehen tagsüber und während den Mahlzeiten zur freien Verfügung.

Es wird in 3-6-Bettzimmern in Etagenbetten geschlafen. Jedes Zimmer mit Duschbad/WC.

Wir bieten
Surf- und Segelkurse,
auch für Anfänger,
mit abschließender Prüfung
(falls erwünscht).
Preise: € 650,– (1 Woche),
€ 1100,– (2 Wochen),
€ 1500,– (3 Wochen),

Unterkunft und Verpflegung einschl. Unterrichtsgebühr, zusätzlich Prüfungsgebühren (Grundschein Windsurfen € 40,–, Grundschein Segeln € 65,–).

Alle unsere Trainer sprechen gut Englisch (zwei außerdem noch Dänisch), da wir oft TeilnehmerInnen aus Skandinavien oder Polen haben.

You can start like this:

> Dear Chris
> You wrote that you were looking for a summer school for water sports in Germany.
> …
> Yours

■ **TIP**

Remember to check your spelling. Even English words used in German often have a different spelling in English, e.g. ein **T**eenager but a **t**eenager.

Going Places Chapter 4 53

Focus on Literature

▶ S8: Reading, watching and analysing drama, WB pp. 64–66

Drama

1 Reading a script

SB A ◀

These are the initial stage directions for Alfred Uhry's play *Driving Miss Daisy* (1987).

> *In the dark we hear a car ignition turn on, and then a horrible crash. Bangs and booms and wood splintering. When the noise is very loud, it stops suddenly and the lights come up on Daisy Werthan's living room, or a portion thereof. Daisy, age 72, is wearing a summer dress and high heeled shoes. Her hair, her clothes, her walk, everything about her suggests bristle and feistiness and high energy. She appears to be in excellent health. Her son, Boolie Werthan, 40, is a businessman, Junior Chamber of Commerce style. He has a strong, capable air. [...]*

1 **ignition** starting device
4 **bristle** anger
feistiness determination
5/6 **Junior Chamber of Commerce style** *here:* demonstrating success

a A play is meant to be performed, not read: make notes on what you would hear and see at the beginning of the play in a theatre performance.

b While reading the first dialogue of the play below, try to imagine the scene behind the words. Think about these questions:

1 Where are Daisy and Boolie positioned in the living room (i.e. on the stage)?

2 Are they sitting or standing? Moving around or standing still? (Perhaps they change their postures during parts of the scene?)

3 How close together do they get?

4 What kind of furniture can you 'see' in the living room?

Daisy: No!
Boolie: Mama!
Daisy: No!
Boolie: Mama!
Daisy: I said no, Boolie, and that's the end of it.
Boolie: It's a miracle you're not laying in Emory Hospital – or decked out at the funeral home. Look at you! You didn't even break your glasses.
Daisy: It was the car's fault.
Boolie: Mama, the car didn't just back over the driveway and land on the Pollard's garage all by itself. You had it in the wrong gear.
Daisy: I did not!
Boolie: You put it in reverse instead of drive. The police report shows that.
Daisy: You should have let me keep my La Salle.
Boolie: Your La Salle was eight years old.
Daisy: I don't care. It never would have behaved this way. And you know it.
Boolie: Mama, cars don't behave. They are behaved upon. The fact is you, all by yourself, demolished that Packard.
Daisy: Think what you want. I know the truth.
Boolie: The truth is you shouldn't be allowed to drive a car any more.
Daisy: No.

6 **laying** *(slang)* = lying
decked out: *aufgebahrt*
13/17 **La Salle, Packard** brand names of cars

54
Focus on Literature

Drama

Boolie: Mama, we are just going to have to hire somebody to drive you.
Daisy: No we are not. This is my business.
Boolie: Your insurance policy is written so that they are going to have to give you a brand new car.
Daisy: Not another Packard, I hope.
25 **Boolie:** Lord Almighty! Don't you see what I'm saying?
Daisy: Quit talking so ugly to your mother.
Boolie: Mama, you are seventy-two years old and you just cost the insurance company twenty-seven hundred dollars. You are a terrible risk. Nobody is going to issue you a policy after this.
30 **Daisy:** You're just saying that to be hateful.
Boolie: O.K. Yes. Yes I am. I'm making it all up. Every insurance company in America is lined up in the driveway waving their fountain pens and falling all over themselves to get you to sign on. Everybody wants Daisy Werthan, the only woman in the history of driving to demolish a three week old Packard, a two car garage and a free standing tool shed in one fell swoop!
35 **Daisy:** You talk so foolish sometimes, Boolie.
[…]

From: Alfred Uhry, *Driving Miss Daisy*, © 1986 by Alfred Uhry

28 **issue sb. a policy** einen Versicherungsschein ausstellen
32 **fountain pen** *Füller*
34 **in one fell swoop** in a single action

c Insert some stage directions to illustrate your mental image of the scene (cf. SB p. 108).

2 Looking at the content   SB B ◀

a Describe the two characters, mother and son, as you see them in the scene. Choose three adjectives you think fit each character best and add short notes to explain your choice.

b Tick the sentences you think best describe the relationship between mother and son in this scene (one from each perspective).

1. ☐ Boolie wants to decide how his aging mother should live.
2. ☐ Boolie is trying to persuade his mother to realize she needs help.
3. ☐ Boolie is afraid that his mother's behaviour will cost too much money.
4. ☐ Daisy does not want to lose her independence.
5. ☐ Daisy is angry that her son thinks he knows what's best for his mother.
6. ☐ Daisy is beginning to understand that Boolie is right.

c **CHALLENGE** Imagine either character (Daisy or Boolie) talking about the accident and the following conversation to a friend (or, in Boolie's case, to his wife). Make up a dialogue.

> **Daisy:** guess what happened … • accident • you'll never believe … • that awful Packard • good riddance! • unthinkable • stranger • my life – …
> **Boolie:** stubborn as hell • can't make her see • terribly naïve • makes me worry • insurance policy • new car • won't see reason • something has to be done • a danger to herself and others • …

aggressive • arrogant • bossy • cheerful • determined • dignified • excitable • foolish • frustrated • hateful • hysterical • ironic • naïve • polite • relaxed • senile • stubborn

3 Understanding dramatic conflict   SB B ◀

a Say what you think the dramatic conflict will be in *Driving Miss Daisy*. Your answers to question **2b** should help you here.

b Compare the opening scenes from *Multiple Choice* (SB pp. 108–109) and *Driving Miss Daisy* with regard to the dramatic conflict. Choose adjectives from the box below that fit your view of the atmosphere in each extract, and decide which ones create more tension. Finish by writing a short explanation in your exercise book.

> aggressive • angry • awkward • calm • excited • frustrated • indifferent • open • polite • secretive • upset • worried

Focus on Literature

Skills Practice

Skills File	WB exercises
Listening and viewing skills	pp. 56–57
Reading and text skills	pp. 57–68
Speaking skills	pp. 69–72
Writing skills	pp. 72–81
Mediation skills	pp. 81–83
Study skills	pp. 84–91

Listening and viewing skills

▶ S1 Listening for information   SB p. 120 ◀

Listening for gist is like skimming a written text. You use it when you need to have a general idea of what a spoken text is about.

You can download this audio file and transcript here:

Webcode starwb-09

1 Resurrection
You are interested in future developments in science. You have gone onto *The Economist*'s website and have found an item called 'Resurrection'. Listen to the text.

a **Before listening:** Speculate on what the title could refer to.

_____

_____

b **While listening:** Answer the following questions.
   1 Who is speaking? Tick the correct box.
      a ☐ a panel of experts
      b ☐ two editors from *The Economist*
      c ☐ an editor from *The Economist* and an expert on scientific affairs

   2 What are they talking about? Tick <u>two</u> boxes.
      a ☐ Tyrrhenian eye-bags, a type of Mediterranean fish
      b ☐ an extinct frog in Australia
      c ☐ a new kind of radar
      d ☐ the threat to Australia of a fog of poisonous gas
      e ☐ the ibex, a species of wild goat found in the Spanish Pyrenees
      f ☐ the contribution of freezers to global warming

   3 Which of the following key words occur in the text? <u>Underline</u> the correct word in each group.
      a   alterations   alternations   alternatives
      b   BNP   DCA   DNA
      c   extinct   extract
      d   genes   genomes   gnomes
      e   species   speeches
      f   technology   biology

S3 • Reading and text skills

c **After listening:** Summarize what 'Resurrection' is about in 20–40 words.

_____
_____
_____
_____

> Often listening for gist is not enough. You my also have to **listen for detail** to find out specific information. Taking notes is frequently an important skill when doing this.

2 The Rosetta mission
Listen to the text twice, first for gist, then for detail.

a **First listening:** Tick the correct box in each question.
1. Churyumov-Gerasimenko is the name of …
   a ☐ the archaeologist who discovered the Rosetta Stone.
   b ☐ the Ukrainian-American scientist who planned the space mission to a comet.
   c ☐ the name of a comet which is the destination of a European space mission.

2. What is the aim of the Rosetta mission?
   a ☐ To determine why the previous US mission failed.
   b ☐ To look at a comet in greater detail.
   c ☐ To find out how ancient languages are related.

b **Second listening:** Now answer briefly these more detailed questions.
1. How is Rosetta different from previous missions?

_____
_____
_____

2. Why is the information scientists hope to gather important?

_____
_____
_____

You can download this audio file and transcript here:
Webcode starwb-10

▶ S22: Making and taking notes, WB p. 84

Reading and text skills

▶ S3 Marking up a text   SB pp. 122–123 ◀

This is a skill that is useful for many different tasks, e.g. mediating, or writing a summary. You can practise this skill in the exercises listed on the right.

- ▶ S7: Reading and analysing narrative prose, exercise 5a, WB p. 61
- ▶ S9: Reading and analysing poetry, exercise 14a, WB p. 68
- ▶ S17: Argumentative writing, exercise 24a, WB p. 76
- ▶ S18: Writing a review, exercise 25a, WB p. 77
- ▶ S20: Writing a summary, exercise 27a, WB p. 79
- ▶ S21: Mediation of written and oral texts, exercises 28/29, WB pp. 81–83

Skills Practice

S5 • Reading and text skills

▶ S5 Identifying text types

SB pp. 124–125 ◀

This is an important skill as it is the first step towards analysing texts systematically.

3 Expository, descriptive, argumentative, persuasive or instructive?
Compare the four text excerpts below. Read the information on SB pp. 124–125, then decide which text type each excerpt represents. Explain your answers briefly.

A

Obama's report gives the lie to Britain's timid platitudes: a debate is possible

What a relief. It is, after all, possible to discuss the operations of modern intelligence agencies without having to prove one's patriotism, be turned over by the police, summoned by politicians or visited by state-employed technicians with instructions to smash up one's computers.

The 300-page report into *The Guardian's* revelations about the US National Security Agency commissioned by President Obama and published this week is wide-ranging, informed and thoughtful. It leaps beyond the timid privacy-versus-national security platitudes which have stifled so much of the debate in the UK. It doesn't blame journalism for dragging the subject into the open: it celebrates it.

The five authors of the report are not hand-wringing liberals. They number one former CIA deputy director; a counter-terrorism adviser to George W Bush and his father; two former White House advisers; and a former dean of the Chicago law school. Not what the prime minister would call "airy-fairy lah-di-dah" types.

Source: Alan Rusbridger, *The Guardian*, 20 December 2013

Text type: _____
Reason(s): _____

B

A letter to … My 'best friend'

I know now that I should have chosen my friends more carefully but at the age of 12, friendships are rather arbitrary, aren't they? In any case, I didn't do the choosing, did I? You chose me. You were pretty, vivacious and charming and I, poor little fool, was flattered that you wanted me as a companion. [...]

To my amazement our class's number one alpha male started dating shy, mousy little me instead of you. We went out together for several years. When we eventually married, were you jealous? It didn't occur to me that you would be. I thought that you were immune to his good looks, charisma and his smart-arse humour – I suspected that they were competition for your own. You made disparaging remarks about his arrogance, his cockiness and the way he dominated social situations. I thought you didn't like him.

Source: *The Guardian*, Family section, 5 October 2013

Text type: _____
Reason(s): _____

Margin glossary:
- 6 **platitude** comment or statement that has been made often before and is therefore not interesting
- 6 **stifle sth.** ['staɪfl] *etw. ersticken*
- 9 **hand-wringing** oversensitive
- 12 **airy-fairy** *infml* not practical, unclear
- **lah-di-dah** *infml* not natural or sincere

- 3 **vivacious** [vɪ'veɪʃəs] very lively
- 5 **alpha male** man in a group who has the most power
- 8 **smart-arse** *slang* showing off
- 9 **disparaging** [dɪs'pærədʒɪŋ] *abschätzig*
- **cockiness** overconfidence

58 Skills Practice

S5 · Reading and text skills

C

My 250 texts a day

I ask a teenage girl, how often do you text? "250 times a day, or something," she tells me. Shocking! The digital lives of teenagers have become the target of weekly attacks. In a recent essay for *The Guardian*, the novelist Jonathan Franzen bemoaned online socialising, arguing that it was creating a uniquely shallow and trivial culture, making kids unable to socialise face to face. Then the American comedian Louis CK proclaimed on TV that he wouldn't give his daughters cellphones for fear they wouldn't develop empathy. [...]

The trend is real. Is it, as Franzen and the others fear, turning kids into emotion-addled zombies, unable to connect, unable to think, form a coherent thought or even make eye contact? Could this be true?

I don't think so. Let's go back to that girl who texts 250 times a day. The truth is, she was an extreme case I cherry-picked to startle you – because when I interviewed her, she was in a group of friends with a much wider range of experiences. Two others said they text only 10 times a day. One was a Facebook refusenik [...]. A few were devotees of Snapchat, the app that lets you send a picture or text that, like a cold-war communiqué, is destroyed after one viewing. [...] As it turns out, the diversity of use in this group of friends is confirmed by research. Fewer than 20% of kids send more than 200 texts a day; 31% send 20 or fewer.

Source: Clive Thompson, *The Guardian*, Family section, 5 October 2013

- 3 **bemoan sth.** complain about sth.
- 4 **shallow** seicht, oberflächlich
- 11 **cherry-pick sth.** die Rosinen herauspicken
- 13 **refusenik** [rɪˈfjuːznɪk] Verweigerer

Text type: _____

Reason(s): _____

D

Economic crisis leads to 1.3% fall in carbon emissions

Global emissions of carbon dioxide dropped by 1.3% in 2009 compared with the previous year, largely due to the effects of the economic crisis and an overall fall in GDP, according to an international team of scientists.

The drop is smaller than the 2.8% fall predicted by many experts for 2009, however, because the reductions in carbon emissions per unit of GDP – a measure of efficiency called the carbon intensity – was smaller than expected in many emerging economies.

Source: Alok Jha, *The Guardian*, 22 November 2013

Text type: _____

Reason(s): _____

Skills Practice

S6 Reading and analysing non-fiction

SB p. 126

Reading non-fiction texts is very important. In contrast to fiction, where the main emphasis is on the world created by the author's imagination, a non-fiction text contains facts that can be checked. This type of text is also used to express opinions.

4 'The Summer of the Shark'

a Read the text below and decide what text type it is. _____

Cast an eye back for a moment to the summer months of 2001, which in the United States came to be known as the Summer of the Shark. The media brought us chilling tales of rampant shark carnage. The prime example was the story of Jessie Arbogast, an eight-year-old boy who was playing in the warm, shallow Gulf waves of Pensacola, Florida, when a bull shark ripped off his right arm and gorged a big piece of his thigh as well. *Time* magazine ran a cover package about shark attacks. Here is the lead of the main article:

> Sharks come silently, without warning. There are three ways they strike: the hit-and-run, the bump-and-bite and the sneak attack. The hit-and-run is the most common. The shark may see the sole of a swimmer's foot, think it's a fish and take a bite before realizing this isn't its usual prey.

Scared yet?

A reasonable person might never go near the ocean again. But how many shark attacks do you think actually happened that year?

Take a guess – and then cut your guess in half, and now cut it in half a few more times. During the entire year of 2001, around the world there were just 68 shark attacks, of which 4 were fatal.

Not only are these numbers far lower than the media hysteria implied; they were also no higher than in earlier years or in the years to follow. Between 1995 and 2005, there were on average 60.3 worldwide shark attacks each year, with a high of 79 and a low of 46. There were on average 5.9 fatalities per year, with a high of 11 and a low of 3. In other words, the headlines during the summer of 2001 might just as easily have read "Shark Attacks About Average This Year." But that probably wouldn't have sold many magazines.

So for a moment, instead of thinking about poor Jessie Arbogast and the tragedy he and his family faced, think of this: in a world with more than 6 billion people, only 4 of them died in 2001 from shark attacks. More people are probably run over by TV news vans.

Elephants, meanwhile, kill at least 200 people every year. So why aren't we petrified of them? Probably because most of their victims live in places far from the world's media centers. It may also have something to do with the perceptions we glean from the movies. Friendly, entertaining elephants are a staple of children's films (think *Babar* and *Dumbo*); sharks, meanwhile, are inevitably typecast as villains. If sharks had any legal connections whatsoever, they surely would have sued for an injunction against *Jaws*.

Source: Steven D. Levitt, Stephen J. Dubner, *Superfreakonomics*. New York, HarperCollins, 2006

▶ S5: Identifying text types, WB pp. 58–59

b Summarize the content of the excerpt in 1–2 sentences.

_____
_____
_____

▶ S20: Writing a summary, WB pp. 79–81

c How do the writers make the text interesting? Check the information on SB p. 126 again, especially the sections on argumentation and stylistic devices.

d What feelings do the authors want to evoke in the reader in this text? Choose one of the emotions in the box and explain why you chose it.

anger • curiosity • excitement • fear • happiness • pride • satisfaction • sympathy

S7 • Reading and text skills

▶ S7 Reading and analysing narrative prose   SB p.127 ◀

When we talk about reading or analysing narrative prose, we usually refer to novels or short stories. The following extracts are from a short story, but they provide elements that you could find in a novel as well.

5 Gathering information and anticipating plot

After being arrested for smoking a joint and rioting in the street with some friends, 16-year-old Shane, who lives in Anaheim, California, with his grandparents, gets an invitation to spend the summer vacation in Mendocino, Northern California, with his mother Susan and her new partner, Roy Bentley. He doesn't want to go, but his grandparents think it will be good for him and make him accept.

> The scene at the airport was as difficult as he feared it might be. His grandmother started sniffling, and then his grandfather went through a big hugging routine, and then Shane himself had to repress a terrible urge to cry. He was glad when the car pulled away, taking two white heads with it. In the coffee shop, he drank a coke and swallowed a couple of 'ludes to calm his nerves. As the pills took hold, he
> 5 began to be impressed by the interior of the terminal. It seemed very slick and shiny, hard-surfaced, with light bouncing around everywhere. The heels of people's shoes caused a lot of noise.
>   Susan had enclosed a snapshot with her check, and Shane removed it from his wallet to study it again. It showed his mother and Roy Bentley posed on the deck of their house. Bentley was skinny, sparsely bearded, with rotten teeth. He looked more like a dope dealer than a manufacturer. Shane figured that
> 10 he probably farmed marijuana in Mendocino, where sinsemilla grew with such astounding energy that it made millionaires out of extremely improbable types. [...]
>
> From: 'Hard to Be Good' by Bill Barich, from *The New Yorker* 1982, reprinted in *The Year's Best American Short Stories*, ed. Anne Tyler with Shannon Ravenel, London: Severn House, 1984

4 **'ludes** Quaaludes: brand name for a sedative drug called Methaqualone
10 **sinsemilla** a very potent form of marijuana

a Read the extract and outline what information about Shane you get from it. Mark the relevant phrases in the text and make notes either in the margin or in your exercise book.

_____

_____

▶ S3: Marking up a text, SB pp.122–123
▶ S22: Making and taking notes, WB p.84

b Point out what information is given about the other characters.

_____

_____

_____

c Speculate what kind of plot can be expected from the information given so far, including the title.

_____

_____

_____

6 Identifying the narrator and the point of view

a Analyse the text with regard to who is giving the information you have gathered, and from whose point of view it is being given.

_____

_____

▶ Narrative Prose – the Short Story, Part B, SB p.58

Skills Practice

S7 • Reading and text skills

b Explain the effect of this particular point of view. You might first want to imagine that the situation was narrated from a different point of view (perhaps a neutral observer of the scene at the airport) in order to see the effect better.

_____

_____

_____

7 Examining plot development

Shane gradually adapts to life on the ranch, and even enjoys working in Roy Bentley's factory packing plastic duck-shaped lamps. Instead of wages, Bentley has promised to give him an old Chrysler which he keeps in a barn, provided he can pass his driver's test.

> Shane's driving test was scheduled for a Thursday afternoon. Bentley gave him permission to come home early from work to practice. He backed the Chrysler into the barn several times without scratching it, and then he walked over to the house, hoping that Susan would make him a snack, but she'd gone to town for her yoga class. The phone rang while he was eating a boiled hot dog. Darren Grady was on the line, calling from Elk, a town south of Medocino. Grady was upset, distressed, talking a mile a minute. He'd run away from the seminary. He was stranded, broke. Shane couldn't believe it. Where had Grady's wisdom gone? "Take it easy, Darren," he said. "Everything's going to be all right."
>
> But Grady was blubbering. "I was trying to hitch to your place," he said, "but this highway patrol, he kicked me off the road. I cooled it in the bushes for a while and tried again, but here comes old highway patrol with his flasher on. I gave him the finger and split for town. I'm like a hunted criminal, Shane. You got to help me."
>
> Shane glanced at the kitchen clock. He figured that he could get to Elk and back before he and Bentley were scheduled to meet the state examiner, so he told Grady to sit tight. The drive over there took about twenty minutes and gave him a severe case of paranoia. Every car that approached him seemed from a distance to be black and ominous and full of cops. [...]

It turns out that Darren has been drinking and still has a few cans of beer on him when he gets into Shane's car. When he throws an empty can out into the road, it arouses the interest of a policeman waiting at the side of a road for speeders. He pursues Shane's car.

> Grady sank lower in the seat. "I'm holding, Shane," he said morosely. Shane didn't want to take his eyes from the road. "You're *what*?"
>
> "I'm holding some speed. I bought it at that arcade." He showed Shane four pills. "Should I throw them out the window?"
>
> The pills got swallowed – Shane couldn't think of any other way to dispose of them. He and Grady ate two apiece, which lent a hallucinatory edge to subsequent events. [...]
>
> From: 'Hard to Be Good' by Bill Barich, from *The New Yorker* 1982, reprinted in *The Year's Best American Short Stories*, ed. Anne Tyler with Shannon Ravenel, London: Severn House, 1984

a List the events of that Thursday afternoon in chronological order.

_____

_____

_____

_____

_____

---

5 **Darren** a young man Shane made friends with on the plane; he was on his way to join a religious brotherhood because he had had a vision telling him he needed to save his soul

3 **speed** amphetamine: a drug

▶ S22: Making and taking notes, WB p. 84

Skills Practice

S7 • Reading and text skills

b Speculate on the 'subsequent events' mentioned in the last line of the extract.

_____

_____

_____

c Analyse how the events you have listed are linked to each other as well as to the driving test mentioned in the first sentence of the extract in order to make up the plot.

d **CHALLENGE** Write a short comment in answer to the following question: 'Should Shane have denied his friend the help he was asking for and gone to his driving test instead?'

8 Analysing the ending of a story

The following is the last paragraph of the story. While reading it, try to imagine what must have happened between the Thursday you read about earlier and this morning in late August.

> In late August, there was an unseasonal thunderstorm. It rattled windowpanes and made chickens flap in their coops. When it was over, the morning sky was clear and absolutely free of fog. Shane got up early and changed the oil in the Chrysler. He filled the trunk with his belongings and put a pair of ducks for the Harrises on the back seat. Susan was not entirely recovered from her surgery,
> 5 so he had to say goodbye to her in her bedroom, where she was propped up against pillows. She asked him again if he didn't want to transfer to a school in Medocino and stay on with them, but he told her that he missed his grandparents and his friends. "I might come back next summer," he said, kissing her on the cheek. "You'll probably have the baby by then." Bentley stuck fifty dollars in the pocket of his jeans. "You ain't such a bad apple, after all," said Bentley with a smile. Shane drove off
> 10 quickly, without looking back. The highway was still slick and wet from the rain, and the scent of eucalyptus was in the air.
>
> From: 'Hard to Be Good' by Bill Barich, from *The New Yorker* 1982, reprinted in *The Year's Best American Short Stories*, ed. Anne Tyler with Shannon Ravenel, London: Severn House, 1984

2 free of fog
northern California is known for its mist and fog, especially in the mornings

4 the Harrises
Shane's grandparents

a Mark the parts of the text that hint at how Shane's visit with his mother and Roy Bentley continued, and list the developments that you can guess at.

_____

_____

_____

_____

▶ S22: Making and taking notes, WB p. 84

b The first two sentences and the last sentence of the extract deal with weather or other natural phenomena. What connotations do you think they have and how do these to the rest of the story?

1 thunderstorm _____

2 rattle windowpanes _____

3 make chickens flap in their coops _____

4 clear sky _____

5 free of fog _____

6 the highway was still slick and wet from the rain _____

7 scent of eucalyptus in the air _____

c On the basis of your analysis, write a short interpretation of the final paragraph.

Skills Practice

63

S8 • Reading and text skills

▶ S8 Reading, watching and analysing drama
SB pp. 127–128 ◀

Plays are meant to be performed, so when you are reading the text of a play, imagine what you would probably see and hear when watching it in a theatre.

9 Constructing plot from dialogue

You are going to read an extract from a play about ZeeBoy, a Superhero made almost completely of metal and running on batteries, from the planet Zola. He fled his planet because he was being pursued by the army, which wanted to recruit him. He owns a watch with special powers that helped him leave his planet and now gives him information when he does not understand what is going on. On his flight from Zola to Earth he ran right into a pre-Olympic race organized by a sports academy that is training young people for the Olympics; having outrun everyone else he is now the new champion, but nobody knows that he is different from anybody else on earth.

a While reading the extract make notes on the following questions:
1 What are the two kids talking about?

2 What does Kalina believe about ZeeBoy's past?

3 What is ZeeBoy's problem in the new situation?

4 What does he do to solve it?

▶ S22: Making and taking notes, WB p. 84

3 **beat** *here:* short pause (as of one heartbeat)
17 **geek** *Streber, Computerfreak*

ZeeBoy:	Hi.
Kalina:	Hi.
Beat	
	You just beat everyone. I wish I had your talent.
ZeeBoy:	Who says you haven't?
Kalina:	I always come in third place. Never won a single race.
ZeeBoy:	I could help take you from third to first place.
Kalina:	What? Train together?
ZeeBoy:	Yes.
Kalina:	I'd like that. You know I'm not bothered which country you're from.
ZeeBoy:	Or … planet?
Kalina:	*(nervously carries on rambling)* I mean I've never met a real refugee. It must be kind of weird for you, maybe weird's not the right word – tragic? Or maybe it's brilliant that you've kind of escaped? Or both? Tragic and brilliant, with a bit of weird thrown in there? *(Beat)* I can be weird too!
Awkward pause	
	(Pointing at **Marvel***)* That's my brother Marvel, so I'm kinda used to geeks trying to be superheroes.
ZeeBoy:	You have superheroes here?
Kalina:	We have superhero worshippers. Take my brother: he's ten years old and changed his name to Marvel, after his favourite comic-book series.
ZeeBoy:	And a comic book holds the life story to all superheroes?
Kalina:	Yeah, suppose so.
ZeeBoy:	What was everyone cheering for back there?
Kalina:	Duh, for you?

5

10

15

20

25

Skills Practice

	ZeeBoy:	Me? What do you know? What have I done? Are they here to take me away?
	Kalina:	Hey, it's okay. You're safe here.
	ZeeBoy:	Am I?
	Kalina:	Yeah.
30	*Pause*	
	ZeeBoy:	Back home there's a war going on, our enemies have created a Super Enemy and everyone my age is being forced into the army to fight a war, but we just want to be …
	Kalina:	Kids?
	ZeeBoy:	Yes. I no longer want to be a Su---
35	**Kalina:**	It's cool – you don't need to explain anything. Unfortunately this academy will train you as hard as the army, but at least there's no war to worry about. You got somewhere to sleep?
	ZeeBoy:	I have a twenty-four-hour battery. So I don't really need to sleep.
	Kalina:	You're kind of odd. I like you. Your battery will have to be at the max as you're our Olympic hero and tomorrow's the big day.
40	**ZeeBoy:**	I am an Olympic hero?
	Kalina:	Do you know anything about anything?
	ZeeBoy:	Can I just go to the …
	Kalina:	Toilet?
45	**ZeeBoy** *walks to a quiet spot and speaks to his watch.*	
	ZeeBoy:	Watch. Olympic history, please.
	[…]	

From: *So You Think You're a Superhero?* by Parven Virk in *National Theatre Connections 2012.* Plays for young people. Methuen Drama 2012

39 **at the max**
the maximum performance

b Write what the extract is about in one or two sentences.

c Speculate on what the dramatic conflict will be about and what might happen in the course of ZeeBoy's stay in the sports academy.

10 Misunderstandings

a Look at the extract again and study the passages in which Kalina and ZeeBoy do not really understand each other because their connotations of the words *planet*, *superhero* and *battery* are different (ll. 10–15; ll. 18–23, ll. 38–40), and explain what each of them means.

S9 • Reading and text skills

b Explain the irony in Kalina's use of the word 'weird' in ll. 12–15: what does she mean when she says 'I can be weird too', and why would the audience probably laugh at her words?

_____
_____
_____
_____

c Describe the character of Kalina as you see her in this extract. The words in the box on the left may help you.

> eager • friendly
> • frustrated •
> helpful •
> outgoing •
> puzzled •
> talkative

_____
_____
_____

11 Stage directions and props

a Identify the stage directions in the text and explain how they help us to understand the action.

_____
_____
_____
_____
_____
_____

b Add new stage directions of your own in three places where you think they might help the actors perform. Include tone of voice and body language in your stage directions. 📝

c List items that you would expect to see on the stage during a performance of the scene. 📝

▶ S9 Reading and analysing poetry   SB pp. 128–129 ◀

When reading and analysing poems, you will often be asked to identify images that the poet uses.

12 Painting images with words

You are going to read a poem (p. 67) by the American writer, editor and poet, Joyce Kilmer (1886–1918), who was killed at the end of the First World War.

If possible, read it aloud to yourself, to get a feeling for its rhythm and content. While reading, try to 'see' in your mind the central image that the poet is painting with his words.
Write in one or two sentences what the poem is about. Say what mental image(s) you had while reading it.

_____
_____
_____
_____
_____

The House with Nobody in It

WHENEVER I walk to Suffern along the Erie track
I go by a poor old farmhouse with its shingles broken and black.
I suppose I've passed it a hundred times, but I always stop for a minute
And look at the house, the tragic house, the house with nobody in it.

5 I never have seen a haunted house, but I hear there are such things;
That they hold the talk of spirits, their mirth and sorrowings.
I know this house isn't haunted, and I wish it were, I do;
For it wouldn't be so lonely if it had a ghost or two.

This house on the road to Suffern needs a dozen panes of glass,
10 And somebody ought to weed the walk and take a scythe to the grass.
It needs new paint and shingles, and the vines should be trimmed and tied;
But what it needs the most of all is some people living inside.

If I had a lot of money and all my debts were paid
I'd put a gang of men to work with brush and saw and spade.
15 I'd buy that place and fix it up the way it used to be
And I'd find some people who wanted a home and give it to them free.

Now, a new house standing empty, with staring window and door,
Looks idle, perhaps, and foolish, like a hat on its block in the store.
But there's nothing mournful about it; it cannot be sad and lone
20 For the lack of something within it that it has never known.

But a house that has done what a house should do, a house that has sheltered life,
That has put its loving wooden arms around a man and his wife,
A house that has echoed a baby's laugh and held up his stumbling feet,
Is the saddest sight, when it's left alone, that ever your eyes could meet.

25 So whenever I go to Suffern along the Erie track
I never go by the empty house without stopping and looking back,
Yet it hurts me to look at the crumbling roof and the shutters fallen apart,
For I can't help thinking the poor old house is a house with a broken heart.

From: *Trees and Other Poems*, Joyce Kilmer, New York: George H. Doran Company, 1914

13 Examining the structure of the poem.
  a Count the stanzas and determine the rhyme scheme.

  _____

  b Read one or two stanzas aloud again and consider whether the succession of stressed and unstressed syllables is regular or not and how this creates a certain rhythm.

  c Describe the effect of the structural elements that you identified. Tick the statements you think fit your own impression best:
   a ☐ The poem is so regular that it becomes monotonous after a few stanzas.
   b ☐ The poem's regular stanza structure and rhyme scheme give it a flowing effect.
   c ☐ The succession of stressed and unstressed syllables is varied, so that there is a pleasing rhythm of movement.
   d ☐ The lines are of different length, which makes reading the poem aloud rather awkward.
   e ☐ The poem sounds depressing.
   f ☐ The poem sounds lively.
   g ☐ The poem sounds thoughtful.

S9 • Reading and text skills

derelict falling apart, needing repairs

▶ S3: Marking up a text, SB pp. 122–123

14 Examining the stylistic devices
You have now analysed the overall effect of the poem as a work of spoken art. Now it is time to look at images and other stylistic elements (cf. Step 3, SB p. 129).

a **Imagery:** Go through each stanza and mark expressions that describe the house realistically with one colour, and expressions that use elements of description in a metaphorical sense, i.e. with a meaning beyond the straightforward one, with a different colour. Pay special attention to the device of personification.

b Give each stanza a title that contains the word *house* in a suitable way. Pay particular attention to stanza 4 (ll. 13–16), which is the only stanza that does not contain the word *house* itself.

_____

_____

_____

_____

_____

_____

c **Contrasts and repetitions:** Point out the effect of the repetition of the word *house*, which is especially striking in l. 21.

_____

_____

_____

d Analyse the use of contrast in the poem. There is one particularly striking example with several details in ll. 17–24 that you should concentrate on.

_____

_____

_____

e **Special sound devices:** Analyse the effect of alliteration in connection with the other devices you have dealt with. First identify some examples, then find out what they emphasize. 📝

15 The overall development and message of the poem

a Look back at the results of your analysis, including the stanza titles you wrote down, and outline the development of the speaker's thoughts as he repeatedly passes the old farmhouse. It will help you if you focus on linking words like *but*, *for*, *so*, etc. 📝

b The last stanza can be said to contain the climax of the speaker's ideas, which leads to an understanding of the message. In this stanza, the speaker mentions his own feelings for the first time. From the following suggestions, choose the one that you think conveys the overall message of the poem best.
   a ☐ A derelict farmhouse makes the countryside look ugly.
   b ☐ Passing by a derelict house makes you want to start working on it right away.
   c ☐ As long as there are people without a home houses should not be left to fall apart.
   d ☐ When a person has no loved ones left to hold, his heart is broken like a deserted, broken house.

c Write a short explanation of your choice of answer in b. 📝

Skills Practice

Speaking skills

▶ S10 Giving a presentation
SB pp. 130-131

In many areas of your future career, e.g. at university or working for a company or an organization, you will need to do presentations. Presenting a subject clearly and attractively is a useful skill to acquire.

16 Good advice?
You have been given all sorts of tips by friends on how to give a presentation. In each case, say whether you agree or disagree with the advice given below, giving reasons. Check the guidelines on SB pp. 130–131 first.

1 Don't practise your presentation in advance. For a good presentation you need to be spontaneous.

2 Prepare carefully for the presentation by writing out your text in full. Then read it out to your audience so that the message is clear.

3 Don't make your presentation too complicated. Keep it simple.

4 When giving a presentation, you shouldn't use jokes or anecdotes. They only make your audience think you are not being serious.

5 It's not good to use statistics. Most people hate statistics and don't trust them.

6 Don't worry about making mistakes in pronunciation. The context will show what you mean.

7 It's best to avoid eye contact with the audience. They think it looks aggressive if you keep staring at them, and you need to concentrate on reading your notes anyway.

8 Speak more slowly than in normal conversation so that the audience can follow you.

9 Long sentences, lots of statistics and complicated terminology show that you're an expert in the field.

10 If you use PowerPoint slides, put as much information as possible on them. This will help to win the audience over.

11 There's no point in summarizing what you've said at the end. People get bored if you repeat things too much.

12 It's often useful to give people a handout with additional material.

spontaneous
[spɒnˈteɪniəs]
spontan

Skills Practice

S11 • Speaking skills

▶ S11 Communicating in everyday situations

SB pp. 132-133 ◀

Making conversation in a foreign language can be difficult when you are struggling for the right words. In a conversation you are cooperating with someone else, so be helpful, be clear, be polite and friendly. Don't make things difficult for your partner by only giving short answers.

17 Making conversation

a Max is starting a 6-month stay an a British school. His form teacher is talking to him to help him to get used to the unfamiliar surroundings. Read the conversation and think about why it isn't working out. Look at the examples on SB pp. 132–133 for help.

Teacher: Hello Max. How are you settling in?
Max: OK.
Teacher: School in Germany is probably a lot different from here.
Max: Yes.
Teacher: Are you having any problems with understanding things?
Max: No, most of the classes are doing things we did last year in Germany, so I'm a bit bored.
Teacher: Oh, I'm sorry to hear that. How are you getting on with your host family?
Max: They're nice, but I don't like the food.
Teacher: Is there anything particular you don't like?
Max: White bread, fish and chips, beans on toast, steak and kidney pie, drinking tea all day long, roast lamb and mint sauce. Lots.
Teacher: Yes, I'm sure we eat different things than in Germany. Is there anything that you like?
Max: No.
Teacher: Oh dear, well, I hope you get used to things soon.
Max: Yes.
Teacher: Well, I've got to rush. See you on Monday.
Max: Yes.

b Explain what Max did wrong and how he could have improved things.

_____
_____
_____
_____
_____
_____
_____
_____

c Now use some of the phrases from the box below to rewrite the conversation (p. 71) so that it's more polite and works out better.

> I'm afraid • I'm sure • I'm not so keen on • I'm not used to • I'm not so keen on • in general • it looks like • it was nice talking to you • maybe • not really • perhaps I'm wrong • thanks • that's very kind of you, but …

Skills Practice

S12 • Speaking skills

Teacher: Hello Max. How are you settling in?
Max: _____
Teacher: School in Germany is probably a lot different from here.
Max: Yes, _____
_____
Teacher: Are you having any problems with understanding things?
Max: _____
_____
Teacher: Oh, _____ . How are you getting on with your host family?
Max: _____
Teacher: Is there anything particular you don't like?
Max: _____
_____
Teacher: Yes, I'm sure we eat different things than in Germany. Is there anything that you like?
Max: _____
Teacher: Oh dear, well, I hope you get used to things soon.
Max: _____
Teacher: Well, I've got to rush. See you on Monday.
Max: _____

▶ S12 Having a discussion   SB pp. 133-134 ◀

In discussions it is important to be able to agree, disagree and give your opinion politely.

18 I see what you mean, but …

a Put the phrases in the box into the correct lists. Add to the lists if possible.

> Exactly. • I completely agree with you. • I don't agree with you there. • I feel that … •
> If you ask me, … • I'm afraid I can't agree with you. • I'm not sure you're right there. •
> In my opinion, … • I see what you mean, but … • I think (that) … • I think you're right –
> up to a point. • Look at it this way, … • Oh, come on! • The way I see it, …

Agreeing with somebody	Disagreeing with somebody	Giving your opinion

Skills Practice

S13 • Writing skills

b Complete this discussion about the role of money in people's lives, using phrases from **18a**.

Michelle: Money's not my top priority in life. I just don't want to have that worry that I can't fulfil my basic needs.

Tianlin: _____ [1] with you there. For me, a good job and good pay are really important.

Bavleen: _____ [2] : you spent most of your life working, so you need a good job, and I want to be well paid for something I spend most of my life doing. On the other hand, it's not my only priority. _____ [3] , if you let money and your job take over your life, it's no longer your own life.

Justina: _____ [4] ! You've hit the nail on the head, Bavleen. _____ [5] , if you concentrate on having a well paid job, you ignore all sorts of other things, like having a partner and maybe later starting a family.

Tianlin: _____ [6] ! Why does it have to be a case of 'either … or'? Why can't you have both?

Michelle: Basically, _____ [7] you're right, but don't forget that it's very hard to get everything you want: an interesting job, well paid, with a partner you love and a happy family. Just look at all the divorces, or the women – it's usually the women – who have to choose between a family and a career.

Writing skills

▶ S13 The stages of writing   SB p.135 ◀

In any text that you write, it is important that your ideas are in a logical order and that you link them clearly. Carefully planning and revising your text will make it easier for the reader to understand.

19 Using linking words

a Put the linking words and phrases in the box below into the table.

> also • although • as a result • because • but • consequently • e.g. • even if • firstly •
> for example • for instance • however • moreover • secondly • so • therefore • what's more

Functions	Examples
Organizing the text (O)	
Giving reasons (R)	
Adding ideas (A)	
Contrasting thoughts (C)	
Giving examples (E)	
Explaining results and consequences (RC)	

Skills Practice

S14 • Writing skills

b Now divide the text below into separate paragraphs. Then add connectors from the list to improve the text by linking the ideas. The letters in brackets in the text refer to the type of connector that should be used. 📝.

> **TIP**
>
> We divide a text into paragraphs to help the reader to understand the flow of the argument. Each paragraph should contain one basic idea, combined with explanations and examples. Paragraphs should *not* just consist of one or two sentences. Remember also that we indent the beginning of each paragraph to show where the paragraph begins.
> Other useful ways of improving the style of a text are to replace colons or dashes. Using relative clauses is often an improvement, too.

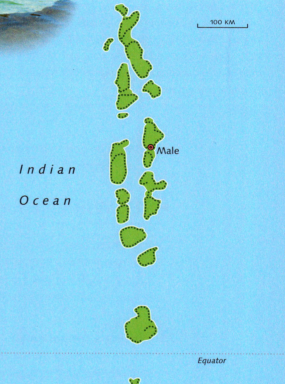

Saving a paradise

(C) Many people in the West see a group of tropical islands like the Maldives as a paradise: we are fast destroying that paradise. Scientists have been warning us for many years about global warming. The signs are now clear, even for non-scientists. (O) Experts say we should cut emissions, or half the world will become too hot or too dry for humans. (O) Scientists are now warning: the ice at the poles is melting much faster than expected. (RC) A group of islands like the Maldives is in danger. They are only 1.5 metres above sea level. (R) Climate change for the Maldives is no longer an abstract danger. (C) It is a real threat to their survival. (A) If the world can't save the Maldives today, it might soon be too late to save low-lying cities – (E) London, New York or Hong Kong tomorrow. (R) Cutting greenhouse gases is important both for faraway islands in the Indian Ocean and for places nearer home.

▶ **S14 Creative writing** SB p. 136 ◀

You may be asked to write a creative text based on an existing text. Creative writing can be fun if you use your imagination, but make sure that you stick to the task that you have been set.

20 Debbie's diary

a Imagine that you are Sara/Debbie in the short story *Debbie's Call* on SB pp. 56–57. When you get home after work, you write about what happened to you in the short story.
Read your diary entry for the previous day first (p. 74), then continue the entry using the words in the vocabulary box.

> a relief • a disaster • aggressive • awful • commuters • crowded bus •
> (to) glance at the manual • (to) lose your job • (to) realize sth. • sth. was wrong •
> (to) swear at sb. • terrible • (to) use the wrong accent

Skills Practice

S15 • Writing skills

Monday 15 April

Today was a pretty ordinary day. Sunil came home as usual at five from school. He was angry because the teacher gave them extra maths homework. I tried to calm him down, but I had to rush off. Didn't want to be late. My job's important to the family. I'm already earning more than Dada does, and we have to pay Sunil's school fees. We also want to move to a bigger place. Today was mainly a clip day – lots of calls from the UK. Everything went smoothly. I slipped into my Sara role – Sara the independent woman, good-looking, super confident. Saw Pavithra in the break. She said, "You're crazy. When I call you on the phone, you even talk like you're still at work. Your life's become one big call centre." She's right, of course, but it's a good way of escaping from the heat and dust of Mumbai. And it doesn't do any harm, does it?

Tuesday 16 April

Today was awful. ...

b What do you think you will be doing in 20 years' time? Describe your job, your family and your home.

▶ S15 Writing a formal letter or email   SB pp. 136–137 ◀

> We use formal letters or emails when we communicate with people we do not know or where our personal relationship with them is not important in that specific situation.
> Typical examples of this are letters or emails to companies or government offices. Because we do not have face-to-face contact with them, we need to make very clear what we mean.

21 Writing a formal email

Put the paragraphs in the correct order and correct any other mistakes in the mail below. The mail is being sent to Wendy Davies at wendavies@aol.com. Make sure you read the information on SB pp. 136–137 before doing this.

Dear Madam

By the way, is it possible to hire bikes locally?

Could you please also let me know if towels are included in the rent and whether there is parking for two cars.

I wish to confirm that we would like to book Gwyndy Cottage for the first two weeks in July.

I will let you know a few days before we are due to come when we expect to be arriving.

We would be grateful if you could provide us with your bank details so that I can transfer the money for the deposit to your account.

Yours

Skills Practice

S16 Writing an application   SB pp. 137-139

Applications, either for a job or for a place at university, usually consist of two parts:
A **CV** (curriculum vitae), often called a résumé in North America, and a **cover letter**.

22 Writing a CV

a Make notes in the table below about Marietherese Biel.

My name is Marietherese Biel. I am a 22-year-old graduate of the University of Cologne. I was born on 12 January 1992 in Oldenburg, Lower Saxony (Germany). My father is a doctor, my mother is a school teacher. I have two brothers and one sister. I am not married. My nationality is German. My native language is German, but I also speak English fluently (C1). I have a good working knowledge of French and Polish (B1). I also have basic Italian (A2). I studied English as major and French as minor at Cologne from October 2010 to July 2014. I graduated with a Bachelor's degree (2.3 in English and 2.7 in French). In my second year I spent the summer semester of 2012 at the University of Maynooth (Ireland) as part of the Erasmus scheme.
I have been working at the Easytrip Travel Centre, Rylestone, N.S.W. (Australia) since September 2013. My current address is 117 Louee Street, Rylestone, NSW 2798. My phone number is 0061-2-63791058 and my mobile number is 0061-177354796. My e-mail address is m.biel@gmx.de.
I attended Friedrich-Ebert-Gymnasium in Cologne (2001–2010), doing my Abitur there in June 2010, (average: 2.3). I spent July to September travelling around the US. I have also travelled widely within Europe. My interests are dancing, tennis, travel and reading. I am computer literate and familiar with MS Office, Open Office, MS Windows and Linux.
I am a well-motivated, flexible graduate whose aim is to obtain a position as an English-German translator. I worked as a freelance translator for various German firms in the Cologne area from July 2011 to March 2012, and July to October 2012, doing both German-English and English-German translations. While at school I did private tuition in English and French (2007–2009) and worked as a tennis coach at Rodenkirchen Tennis Club (2006–2009).

Education	
2010–2014	
April–June 2012	
2001–2010	
Qualifications/skills	
Language Skills	
IT Skills	
Work experience	
September 2013–present	
July 2011–March 2012, July–October 2012	
2007–2009	
2006–2009	
Hobbies and interests	

▶ S22: Making and taking notes, WB p. 84

b Now write a complete CV for Marietherese.

S17 • Writing skills

23 Writing a cover letter

Marietherese Biel has made notes for a cover letter to go with her application to Ms Penny Ross (Human Resources) for a job (Ref. No. 236) as German-English translator at the Lingua Translation Company, 22 Dobson St., Manchester M3 2ZX. The company needs a native speaker of German with very good English to translate from English to German and to help with some German to English translation work. The job was advertised on the Jobs4U website.

- *native spkr of Gm, extensive experience of E-speaking countries (Australia, Ireland, USA)*
- *suitable for job because: spent total of 11 months translating, companies Cologne area, mostly E-G, but also G-E – worked together with Engl native speaker, several transls*
- *your website: a lot involves work for engineering firms, teaching hospitals*
- *my work: mainly engineering companies, 2 transls for Cologne University Teaching Hospital*
- *more details of experience at interview*
- *for additional info, contact me by email*
- *finish present job 15 June, available for interview from 20 June*

Look at SB pp. 136–137 and then write Marietherese Biel's cover letter to Penny Ross.

▶ S17 Argumentative writing

SB pp. 139-140 ◀

> Writing an essay is a good exercise in organizing your ideas systematically and presenting them in an attractive and coherent way.

24 Globalization: arguments for or against

a Read the text below on globalization and <mark>highlight</mark> the main arguments.

- Globalization and international trade keep prices low and quality high. Countries that try to be self-sufficient and refuse to take part in global markets, find that their businesses become inefficient due to a lack of competition: prices rise, their products lack innovation and they end up with hyperinflation.
- Globalization has led to more inequality in many countries. In South-East Asia, people have experienced tremendous growth over the past couple of decades, but it wasn't spread equally among all the people. The poor have seen a moderate rise in incomes while the wealthy have seen incredible rises in their incomes.
- Globalization can bring wealth to poor countries. For example, much of South-East Asia was very poor a few decades ago; thanks to international trade, many of these countries have experienced huge economic growth. Many of those people are now much better off than their parents were a generation ago.
- Globalization can help bring world peace. As countries become more interconnected, there is a serious incentive for all countries involved to keep the peace. War disturbs international trade and sends stock markets plummeting.
- A single large global market presents certain dangers. If an emerging nation finds itself in financial collapse, it has the potential to bring down most of the world with it. The biggest example of this was the economic downturn experienced across the globe today due to the American banking crisis.
- Globalization can help to protect the environment. In the past a nation like China could produce as much pollution as they like, but today, if China wants to take part in the global market, their trading partners can put pressure on them to clean up their act.
- Globalization always hurts some workers in each country. For example, when NAFTA opened trade with Mexico, US TV factories closed their plants and moved to Mexico for cheaper labour. On the other hand, Mexican farmers can't compete with large American farmers and they are being put out of business.
- Globalization leads to a homogenization of the world's cultures. As nations open up to free trade, they have to accept foreign companies coming into their country and doing business. Some people fear that in time there will cease to be exciting foreign cultures and every nation will be filled with McDonald's and Starbucks.
- Diseases can now spread more easily due to the huge number of people crossing international borders. For example, someone can contract a disease in Asia, such as bird flu and be in the USA within a few hours. In this way they can spread a disease that normally would have killed them before they could reach another country.

b Make notes on the main arguments for and against globalization. Add any other arguments you can think of.

Arguments for globalization	Arguments against globalization
…	…

c Choose three of the arguments and write an essay in your own words, either arguing in favour or against globalization. Read the guidelines on SB pp. 139–141 before you begin.

▶ S22: Making and taking notes, WB p. 84

▶ S13: The stages of writing, WB pp. 72–73

▶ S18 Writing a review
SB pp. 141-142 ◀

A review should contain important information about the book, film or play, but you are also required to express your opinion of the work as well.

25 'Notes From the Midnight Driver'

a Look at the two reviews of a novel. Highlight the important parts of the reviews. Make a note of any vocabulary which might be useful when writing your own review in **d**.

> **TIP**
> Both reviews are taken from the internet. They were not made by professional reviewers. The structure may therefore be different from that normally used by journalists who review books as part of their job.

1 *Notes From the Midnight Driver* is such a laugh-out-loud-until-your-sides-hurt type of funny. This book is about a sixteen-year-old boy named Alex who gets sentenced to volunteer at an old people's home because he was drunk while driving. Once he starts volunteering at the home, he really hates it. The man he must visit with, Mr. Solomon Lewis, is an irritable, stubborn Yiddish man who constantly insults Alex in the foreign language. Alex and Sol (Mr. Lewis) start to build a bridge through Jazz music. Alex brings his guitar with him to visit, and they play together, becoming good friends. But when Alex's sentence time is finished, he feels he cannot leave Sol. In fact, to say good bye, Alex throws a concert in the home and allows Sol to join him and his two friends.

In comparison to other books in this genre, I would say it was one of the best. The characters were all so funny and made this book all the better. I would give this book five out of five stars. It was my favorite bingo book so far. I would probably recommend this book to anyone who likes comedies and likes the realistic fiction genre.

2 The cover of this book is deceptive. I expected it to be silly (it is at times) but I was frankly surprised at the levels of joy and sadness it stirs together. Called a "Tuesdays with Morrie" for teens in the description, I feel like that doesn't do it justice. I am 13 years past my teens and this hit me like a ton of bricks.

I was told in advance by my girlfriend that this book made her laugh and cry, I thought, "yeah I'm sure I'll chuckle, I may get a bit choked up." Long story short, she was right. I had belly laughs, I cried so much she asked if I needed to be alone for a minute. The catch, I knew what was going to happen, from the beginning. I knew who the secret character was from early on, I KNEW but it still got to me. These fictional characters felt real and their emotions passed to me. I sobbed through the final pages unable to remind myself that none of this was real, and yet it felt like it was.

A quick read for a Sunday afternoon in pajamas, but fair warning, have tissues close at hand or your t-shirt is going to have a wet spot on the arm, from the dust that got in your eyes … yeah, dust.

From: http://www.goodreads.com/book/show/547866.Notes_from_the_Midnight_Driver

▶ S3: Marking up a text, SB pp. 122–123

S19 • Writing skills

b Now complete the table below with the information each review gives about the book. (This will help you to compare the two reviews.)

Structure	Review 1	Review 2
Main part: outline of plot, but without the ending		
Comments on plot, characters, dialogue		

c State briefly which of the two reviews is more helpful to you, and why.

_____
_____
_____
_____

d **CHALLENGE** Using the guidelines on SB pp. 141–142, write a review of a book or film you saw recently. The vocabulary you collected in **a** will help you.

▶ S19 Writing a report
SB p. 143 ◀

A report aims to present factual information in a clearly structured way. Writing a report is a useful skill that you may have to use either at university or for your career.

26 The Apollo Theatre

a Read the guidelines on SB p. 143, then use the notes below to write a report about the collapse of a ceiling at the Apollo Theatre in London.

- more than 700 people inside theatre in Shaftesbury Avenue, London's West End, Thursday
- happened 45 minutes after the beginning of a performance of 'The Curious Incident Of The Dog In The Night-Time'
- audience began screaming, part of ceiling collapsed
- 80 people injured
- possible cause: excess water during very heavy downpour
- another explanation: former owner Andrew Lloyd Webber said building in a 'shocking' state 10 years ago and should be demolished, added that English Heritage had opposed this

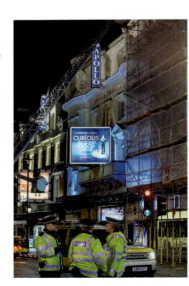

Skills Practice

S20 • Writing skills

b **CHALLENGE** Continue the report by turning the active sentences underlined into passive ones.

1. The emergency services <u>took some of the injured</u> to hospital on board London buses.

2. The hospital <u>discharged most of them</u> shortly afterwards after hospital staff <u>treated them</u> for cuts and bruises.

3. Although the authorities <u>have cancelled performances at the Apollo</u> until 4 January, the London mayor, Boris Johnson, emphasized that the West End was open for business.

4. Many members of the audience <u>praised the rapid response from emergency services</u> as exemplary.

5. The Mayor stressed that Westminster City Council had assured him that experts <u>had made all the necessary safety checks</u> and that they <u>were carrying out additional checks</u> to ensure the safety of other historic theatres in London.

6. A Scotland Yard spokesman said that they <u>were still investigating the matter</u>.

▶ S20 Writing a summary   SB pp. 144-145 ◀

Often people don't have time to read (or listen to) a long text, so they need a summary to save time. In many situations, therefore, you will be expected to make summaries that contain the most important information from the original text. What is important always depends on who you are making the summary for.

27 Summarizing a newspaper report

a Read the newspaper report on p. 80 and ==highlight== the most important information.

▶ S3: Marking up a text, SB pp. 122–123

Kindles help Ghana's reading revolution

[...] Like many schools in Ghana, Suhum has struggled with a chronic lack of textbooks and poor literacy among students. But now, beside the knobbly tree trunks and in the densely packed classrooms, something unusual is happening. Children are sitting down quietly, reading the books of their choice. [...]

"Look at the children. They are playing. It is a sunny day," reads Jessie – a wide-eyed girl with long eyelashes, dimples in her cheeks and hair shaved close to her head. For most schoolgirls in Ghana, long hair is regarded as a privilege for those who have finished school and entered adulthood. Jessie reads aloud, in perfect, softly accented English from a Kindle, the e-reader from online company Amazon, encased in a dark green and blue canvas holder, in which she has proudly written her name in permanent ink to distinguish it from the identical readers of her classmates.

The Kindle gives Jessie access to 140 titles, including textbooks, but mostly stories. *Looking at the Weather* is her favourite. "I really like this story," Jessie says. "The reader makes things better. It helps me to read and spell."

"Now it's easier for my parents to help me with my homework, because I always have the books I need."

The Kindles at Jessie's school have been distributed as part of the iRead 2 programme by Worldreader, a charity conceived by a former Amazon executive and book enthusiast David Risher who, during a volunteer trip at an orphanage in Ecuador, was disturbed to find the library locked and abandoned.

Concerned that children were being deprived of the opportunity to read, Risher created Worldreader to harness the then emerging technology of Kindles – which are less fragile, power hungry and connectivity-dependent than tablets and laptops – to make libraries more accessible. It piloted the project in Ghana – the West African country where, despite strong economic growth and stable democracy, rural areas in particular remain poor. Worldreader now provides Kindles to 3,600 students and their families at 10 schools in Ghana. [...]

"The e-readers are really motivating the students to read," says Kofi Sem Michael, 27, who was inspired to teach by his own experience at school. "It has made the classroom exciting. Everyone has their own book, we can give them reading assignments and they are able to do them." Early results from the project at Suhum show concrete results. At this and other schools in Ghana, Worldreader has found faster reading speeds of an average of five words a minute in the students that have the e-readers than in control schools, as well as 30% faster rates of listening comprehension. [...]

Part of the success of Worldreader seems to be its commitment to pushing local content onto the Kindles, so that the children can access books that relate to their lives. A favourite book of many of the children at Suhum primary school is *Kofi has Malaria*, a story which reflects many of their own experiences with the disease – which is prevalent in Ghana – and educates them about prevention. [...]

"The Kindles have changed the way we teach," said Patrick Kyere-Koranteng, 30, an English teacher at the school. "And in class, if the children don't know a word, now they take the initiative to look it up on the dictionary in the Kindle. The attitude to learning they are developing is going to make a difference through their whole education."

From: Afua Hirsch, *The Guardian*, 13 December 2013

b Note down the main arguments from the text in the table below.

Lines	Arguments
1–2	chronic lack of textbooks, poor literacy in Ghana, e.g. Suhum primary school

▶ S22: Making and taking notes, WP p. 84

c Now use your notes to summarize the report (200–250 words) in your own words as far as possible. Look at the guidelines on SB pp. 144–145 before you begin. These sentence beginning will help you.

Suhum, like many primary schools in Ghana, has had a problem with a severe lack of textbooks and poor student literacy. Jessie …
The Kindles at her school are part of a programme …
Teachers claim that the e-readers help …
The charity points out that using e-readers results in parents becoming …
It explains that the success of Worldreader …

▶ S13: The stages of writing, WB pp. 72–73

Mediation skills

▶ S21 Mediation of written and oral texts   SB pp. 146-147 ◀

Mediation is a skill that is becoming more and more important as international communications increase. As an advanced user of English, you can expect to become involved in situations where you need to mediate between speakers of different languages, e.g. as a tourist abroad, helping foreign tourists in Germany, or summarizing English texts in German for your colleagues or boss.

28 Mediating German to English

As part of a class project on British-German relations your English teacher has asked you to give a short overview of German influences on British Christmas customs. First mark up the text on p. 82, then summarize the important points. Your presentation should not be longer than five minutes. To help you start, the first two sentences have been done for you.

Is Britain's mince pie in danger? The London correspondent of ARD, German television's Channel 1, thinks it is.

Skills Practice

S21 · Mediation skills

> **TIP**
> Check websites in English to find out how to deal with difficult vocabulary. There are also some terms that you will need to explain, e.g. *mince pie*. Marquardt gives a brief description, but you might find it helpful to check this on the internet, too.

Invasion mit Butterstollen

Jedes Land hat seine eigenen, ganz speziellen Weihnachtsbräuche. Einer der wichtigsten in Großbritannien ist eigentlich der Mince Pie, ein mit Brandy oder Rum aromatisiertes Gebäckstück. Doch nun gerät er in Gefahr: Auf Weihnachtsfeiern ist er „out", „in" ist stattdessen Tradition aus Deutschland – der Butterstollen.

By Jens-Peter Marquardt, ARD-Hörfunkstudio London

„Ich habe Stollen probiert – er ist wunderbar. Auf jeden Fall besser als Mince Pie" ... so das Urteil zweier Engländerinnen. Jahrhunderte lang gehörte der Mince Pie zum britischen Weihnachten wie die Geschenke, die durch den Kamin fallen: runde Gebäckstücke, aus Mürbe- oder Blätterteig, mit einer Fruchtfüllung, aromatisiert mit Brandy oder Rum.

Jetzt wird dieses Traditionsgebäck ausgebremst. Auf der Überholspur dagegen: der Weihnachtsstollen. Der Edel-Supermarkt Waitrose meldet aus seinen Filialen einen 50-prozentigen Zuwachs beim Stollenverkauf im Vergleich zu 2012. Sainsbury, nicht ganz so exklusiv, hat den Stollenabsatz um 24 Prozent gesteigert. Und der „Lidl Mini-Marzipan-Butterstollen" ist auf englischen Weihnachtsfeiern zum Renner geworden.

Der Kolumnist des Telegraph gab jetzt zu: „Ein ganzes Leben lang haben wir uns vorgemacht, dass wir Mince Pies mögen. Jetzt merken wir erst, dass wir Marzipan und Stollen eigentlich viel mehr lieben."

Der deutsche Prinz brachte den Weihnachtsbaum mit, ...

Der Siegeszug des Stollens in Großbritannien kommt nicht ganz überraschend: In der Vergangenheit haben immer mehr deutsche Weihnachtsbräuche den Weg über den Kanal gefunden – so zum Beispiel der Weihnachtsbaum. Queen Victorias Ehemann, der deutsche Prinz Albert, stellte 1848 erstmals einen Tannenbaum im Windsor Castle auf.

Das Bild mit Victoria, Albert und den Kindern rund um den geschmückten Baum wurde von allen Zeitungen und Zeitschriften verbreitet und sorgte schnell für Nachahmung: Das britische Volk wollte Weihnachten wie die Royals feiern und stellt seitdem einen Weihnachtsbaum ins Wohnzimmer. Auch das liebste Weihnachtslied der Briten „Silent Night" kommt aus deutscher – oder besser gesagt – österreichischer Produktion.

... die deutsche Partnerstadt den Weihnachtsmarkt

Die eigentliche Invasion aus Deutschland begann allerdings erst vor 13 Jahren: Frankfurt bescherte der Partnerstadt Birmingham einen Weihnachtsmarkt mit 24 Ständen. Dieser Markt wurde zur Erfolgsstory. Heute gibt es dort fast 200 Stände. Busreisen aus dem ganzen Land brachten allein im vergangenen Jahr vier Millionen Besucher auf den „Frankfurt Christmas Market" in Birmingham.

Nicht nur das: Inzwischen gibt es so gut wie keine Stadt mehr in ganz Britannien, die keinen Weihnachtsmarkt hat. London hat gleich mehrere. Im größten, dem Winter-Wonderland im Hyde Park, schieben sich die Massen von der Almhütte zum Bratwurstglöckl, und über allem liegt der Duft von Glühwein und gebrannten Mandeln – zur Freude der Besucher: „Das macht richtig Spaß. Ich finde es sehr weihnachtlich."

... und die deutschen Discounter den Stollen.

Der Mince Pie ist übrigens noch nicht völlig ausgestorben. Er lebt dank deutscher Hilfe weiter. Als die Verbraucherzeitschrift Which? jetzt 12 dieser Traditionsprodukte testete, kam der Mince Pie von Aldi auf Platz eins, der von Lidl auf Platz zwei. Das Londoner Edel-Kaufhaus Fortnum and Mason landete mit seinem – so das Urteil – „ziemlich geschmacklosen" Mince Pie auf dem letzten Platz.

Waitrose versucht derweil dagegen zu halten und die Deutschen auf ihrem ureigenen Terrain zu schlagen: Die britische Supermarktkette hat einen Stollen mit Earl-Grey-Geschmack auf den Markt gebracht.

From: ARD *Tagesschau*, 14 December 2013

Birmingham's Frankfurt Christmas Market

▶ S3: Marking up a text, SB pp. 122–123

▶ S20: Writing a summary, WB pp. 79–81

29 Mediating English to German

Your history class is doing a project on the main historical developments in the last century. You have been asked to give a short talk to explain the spread of English during that period. You have found a good source, but need to summarize it and present it in German. Before writing your summary, highlight the important parts of the text.

English in the 20th century

By 1900, English had been in wide use around the world for over two centuries, but no one could have imagined the communicative and technological support available to it (and to other 'advanced' languages) by 1999. Such developments were in large part the outcome of three sets of events that affected many languages in many ways, and English more than most. These were:

1. Two World Wars (1914–18, 1939–45) in which the key victorious nations were English-speaking. Especially in *World War II* [*AmE* and *BrE*] or the *Second World War* [*BrE*], the use of English for military, political, economic, and other purposes expanded greatly in the various war zones. In Europe, Africa, Asia, and the Pacific millions of people came into regular contact with English who would not otherwise have had much (or anything) to do with it. And where English arrived it tended to stay on after the hostilities ended, for a variety of reasons that included reconstruction, trade, and education.

2. A political and economic Cold War (1945–89) between a capitalist West and a communist East. In this long and often tense struggle for territorial and ideological influence, the USA was the foremost Western contestant. However, after the Soviet Union collapsed in 1989, the USA became the world's only 'super-power', the perceived prestige of which impelled many people in ex-Soviet satellites, such as Czechoslovakia, Hungary, and Poland, to switch from Russian to English as their language of wider communication, having already regarded it for years as a – if not indeed *the* – language of freedom. Inevitably, Russians also began to find it useful to know some English, especially in trying to catch up on a West that was now both technologically and economically far ahead of them.

3. Globalization, the name of a process, set in train after the Soviet collapse, of world-wide social, cultural, and commercial expansion (and exploitation), in which the USA was the *center* [*AmE*] or *centre* [*BrE*] of socio-economic, political, cultural, and linguistic interest. In the closing quarter of the century, English was not only a key socio-cultural language but also the communicative linchpin of both international capitalism and the world's media. By this point, the American variety had also become the main influence not only on other languages but on other Englishes (including the British variety).

From: Tom McArthur, "English World-wide in the Twentieth Century", in: Lynda Mugglestone (ed.), *The Oxford History of English*. Oxford, Oxford University Press, 2012

▶ S3: Marking up a text, SB pp. 122–123
▶ S20: Writing a summary, WB pp. 79–81

Study skills

▶ S22 Making and taking notes
SB p. 148

If you are making or taking notes quickly, you need to make them as short as possible.

30 Decoding abbreviations

a In words it's usually the consonants which give you the most information, not the vowels. Decode these messages:

1 Q here _____
2 C U @ 4 _____
3 Y R U lte? _____
4 Kp it shrt & simpl! _____
5 U dnt nd 2 wrt evry ltr in a wrd 2 B undrstd
_____

b Now use abbreviations to shorten the messages below in the same way.

1 You could ask your teacher. _____
2 Why don't we meet for a coffee? _____
3 Let's have a party. _____
4 What are you getting for Christmas? _____
5 How much homework have you got today? _____

> **TIP**
> You can use the names of English letters and numbers as short forms of words. (You can also use these short forms if you text in English.)
> 2 = to, too, two • 4 = for, four • B = be, bee • C = see, sea • Q = queue • R = are
>
> You can also make up your own abbreviations for common words:
> cd = could • h = have • shd = should • wd = would

▶ S23 Dealing with unknown words
SB p. 149

When you read or hear a new language, there are lots of words whose meaning you won't know. In many cases, however, you can guess their meaning.

31 The Lord above will pay

a Read the extract below from a novel which begins in London in the late 1930s.

Sadie and Jack are Jewish refugees from Nazi Germany, trying to get used to the unfamiliar culture and language of Britain. Jack is taking Sadie by bus to the West End, but the bus is full, so she has to sit downstairs while he finds a seat upstairs. Sadie speaks hardly any English and has no money to pay the conductor.

"Where to, madam?" said the <u>conductor</u>, reaching her seat and <u>jangling</u> his box.
  Sadie gave a <u>timid</u> smile and pointed at the ceiling. "The Lord above, he will pay."
  The conductor <u>spluttered</u> in wordless <u>outrage</u>, and Sadie felt the <u>pudgy</u> woman beside her <u>swivel</u> and stare, the butterflies on her hat <u>wobbling</u> as she <u>sniggered</u>.
  When at home Jack explained her mistake, Sadie couldn't help feeling that the English language was <u>deliberately designed</u> to <u>confound</u> outsiders. 5
  She refused to speak another word to him in that *verdammt* tongue for the rest of the afternoon, and since he would not chat in German, they <u>sulked</u> side by side in silence, until Jack went out. He insisted that they spoke only English […] but speaking with her husband in her <u>disjointed</u> newcomer's tongue transformed him into a stranger. He looked the same, but the easy <u>intimacies</u> were lost. He'd already changed his name. He was Jakob when she fell in love with him, and Jakob when she married him, but when a <u>clerk</u> wrote down 'Jak' on his British visa, he took it as a sign. 10

Source: Natasha Solomons, *Mr Rosenblum's List.* London, Sceptre, 2010

b Guess the meaning of the words underlined in the text on p. 84.

Lines	Help	Meaning
1	Let the context help you if you don't know **conductor** and **jangling**. The conductor is obviously a man who does something on a bus but who is not the driver, because he's going to her seat. He has a box for something, presumably money. The word *jangle* could refer to the noise made by money in a box.	
2	**timid:** There is a similar word in German: '*timide*'. If you don't know what it means, don't worry. Adjectives are not usually key words in a sentence, i.e. you can often understand the basic meaning without them.	
3	The verb **splutter** tells you about the conductor's reaction. *Wordless* shows that he doesn't actually say anything. Is he happy about her not paying? Probably not. You may not know **outrage**, but perhaps you know *rage* in English, or '*Rage*' in German.	
3–4	Is it necessary to understand words like **pudgy**, **swivel**, **wobble** and **snigger**? They give details about the woman's reaction, but how important is she for the basic story?	
5–6	The adverb **deliberately** may not be familiar, but **was designed to** should help you to understand it. If you're not sure what *designed* means, think of the word '*Designer*' in German: someone who '*gestaltet*' things, so *was designed to* means something like '*war so gestaltet, dass …*'. **confound** is a word not often used, but it's similar to a much more frequently used verb beginning with *con-* which fits in this context. Try to guess what it could be, looking at the context. If you know the French word '*confondre*', this will also help.	
8	The situation will help with guessing the meaning of **sulk**. Sadie is angry at Jack because he won't speak German with her, so they both *sulk* in silence.	
9	Because **disjointed** is an adjective it probably isn't essential to the basic meaning. Two elements in the word give a clue to its meaning, though: the prefix *dis-* often means *not* (e.g. *dislike* = *to not like*), and *join* means *connect*.	
10	Can you think of a foreign word in German which is similar to the noun **intimacies**? You may also know the English word *intimate*, which is far more common.	
11	You may not know **clerk**, but it's clear from the context that it refers to an official person.	

Skills Practice

S25 Using a dictionary

SB pp. 151-152

There are lots of problems you can solve when reading English texts without using a dictionary, e.g. by looking carefully at the context. However, a dictionary is often extremely useful because it helps you to find out the meaning and usage of words more accurately.

32 Monolingual or bilingual?

When is it better to use a monolingual dictionary? When is a bilingual one more useful? Tick the right boxes.

A **monolingual** / **bilingual** dictionary is better if you …

a ☐ ☐ want to improve your English vocabulary.
b ☐ ☐ can't think of the English word.
c ☐ ☐ need to have more examples of English words used in a context.
d ☐ ☐ expect the English definition will be too difficult for you to understand.
e ☐ ☐ need to find the English word for '*kosmopolitisch*', but don't understand the German word.

33 Finding out about words

Look at these extracts from the *Oxford Advanced Learner's Dictionary.* Underline or highlight the definition of the words. Then answer the questions on p. 87.

ad·vice /əd'vaɪs/ *noun* [U]
~ **(on sth)** an opinion or a suggestion about what sb should do in a particular situation: *advice on road safety* ◊ *They give advice to people with HIV and AIDS.* ◊ *Ask your teacher's advice/Ask your teacher for advice on how to prepare for an exam.* ◊ *We were advised to seek legal advice.* ◊ *Let me give you a piece of advice.* ◊ *A word of advice. Don't wear that dress.* ◊ *Take my advice. Don't do it.* ◊ *I chose it on his advice.*

con·trast AW *noun, verb*
▪ *noun* /'kɒntrɑːst; NAmE 'kɑːntræst/ **1** [C, U] a difference between two or more people or things that you can see clearly when they are compared or put close together; the fact of comparing two or more things in order to show the differences between them: ~ **(between A and B)** *There is an obvious contrast between the cultures of East and West.* ◊ ~ **(to sb/sth)** *The company lost $7 million this quarter in contrast to a profit of $6.2 million a year earlier.* ◊ *The situation when we arrived was in* **marked contrast** *to the news reports.* ◊ *The poverty of her childhood* **stands in total contrast** *to her life in Hollywood.* ◊ ~ **(with sb/sth)** *to show a* **sharp/stark/striking contrast** *with sth* ◊ ~ **(in sth)** *A wool jacket complements the silk trousers and provides an interesting contrast in texture.* ◊ *When you look at their new system, ours seems very old-fashioned* **by contrast.** ◊ ~ **(of sth)** *Careful contrast of the two plans shows some important differences.* **2** [C, usually sing.] ~ **(to sb/sth)** a person or thing that is clearly different from sb/sth else: *The work you did today is quite a contrast to (= very much better/worse than) what you did last week.* **3** [U] differences in colour or in light and dark, used in photographs and paintings to create a special effect: *The artist's use of contrast is masterly.* **4** [U] the amount of difference between light and dark in a photograph or the picture on a television screen: *Use this button to adjust the contrast.*
▪ *verb* /kən'trɑːst; NAmE -'træst/ **1** [T] ~ **(A and/with B)** to compare two things in order to show the differences between them: *It is interesting to contrast the British legal system with the American one.* ◊ *The poem contrasts youth and age.* **2** [I] ~ **(with sth)** to show a clear difference when close together or when compared: *Her actions contrasted sharply with her promises.* ◊ *Her actions and her promises contrasted sharply.*

eli·gible /'elɪdʒəbl/ *adj.* **1** a person who is **eligible** for sth or to do sth, is able to have or do it because they have the right qualifications, are the right age, etc: ~ **(for sth)** *Only those over 70 are eligible for the special payment.* ◊ (**to do sth**) *When are you eligible to vote in your country?* **OPP** **ineligible** **2** an **eligible** young man or woman is thought to be a good choice as a husband/wife, usually because they are rich or attractive ▶ **eli·gi·bil·ity** /ˌelɪdʒə'bɪləti/ *noun* [U]

get on 1 (also **get along**) used to talk or ask about how well sb is doing in a particular situation: *He's getting on very well at school.* ◊ *How did you get on at the interview?* **2** to be successful in your career, etc: *Parents are always anxious for their children to get on.* ◊ *I don't know how he's going to get on in life.* **3** (also **get a'long**) to manage or survive: *We can get on perfectly well without her.* ◊ *I just can't get along without a secretary.*

host /həʊst; NAmE hoʊst/ *noun, verb*
▪ *noun* **1** [C] a person who invites to a meal, a party, etc. or who has people staying at their house: *Ian, our host, introduced us to the other guests.* ⊃ see also HOSTESS **2** [C] a country, a city or an organization that holds and arranges a special event: *The college is* **playing host** *to a group of visiting Russian scientists.* **3** [C] a person who introduces a television or radio show, and talks to guests **SYN** **compère**: *a TV game show host* ⊃ see also ANNOUNCER, PRESENTER **4** [C] (*technical*) an animal or a plant on which another animal or plant lives and feeds **5** [C] ~ **of sb/sth** a large number of people or things: *a host of possibilities* **6** [C] the main computer in a network that controls or supplies information to other computers that are connected to it: *transferring files from the host to your local computer* **7 the Host** [sing] the bread that is used in the Christian service of COMMUNION, after it has been BLESSED
▪ *verb* **1** ~ **sth** to organize an event to which others are invited and make all the arrangements for them: *South Africa hosted the World Cup finals.* **2** ~ **sth** to introduce a television or radio programme, a show, etc. **SYN** **compère 3** ~ **sth** to organize a party that you have invited guests to: *to host a dinner* **4** ~ **sth** to store a website on a computer connected to the Internet, usually in return for payment: *a company that builds and hosts e-commerce sites*

Source: *Oxford Advanced Learner's Dictionary*, 8th Edition, 2010

Skills Practice

S25 • Study skills

advice
1 What grammatical information is given about the word *advice*? What does [U] mean?

_____

_____

_____

contrast
2 Where is the stress on the noun *contrast* and the verb *to contrast*?

_____

3 How is the pronunciation different in British English and American English? Use phonetic symbols.

	BE	AE
contrast (noun)		
to contrast (verb)		

eligible
4 What does *eligible* mean?

It means being _____

_____

5 Where is the stress on *eligible* and the related noun *eligibility*?

_____

6 How are *eligible* and the related noun *eligibility* pronounced? Use phonetic symbols.

eligible: _____   eligibility: _____

get on
7 What main meanings does this phrasal verb have? Give an example of each use.

a _____

_____

b _____

_____

c _____

_____

8 Where's the stress? _____

host
9 What class of word is *host* in the sentence 'London hosted the Olympics in 2012'? Is it a noun, a verb, or an adjective?

_____

10 What other class of word can *host* be?

_____

_____

11 How is it pronounced, like *cost* or like *most*? Give the phonetic symbols.

_____

_____

Skills Practice

S25 • Study skills

can't be used with an article • different meanings • false friend • idiom • literal translation • the preposition used • refer to • wrong meaning chosen

34 Dein Tee ist im Ofen: popular howlers

a Correct the following translation errors. Use a good bilingual dictionary to help you. Then explain what mistakes have been made. The words in the box will help you to explain the mistakes.

1 Your tea is in the oven. → *Dein Tee ist im Ofen.*

a _____
b _____

2 Wo bekomme ich Hilfe? → *Where do I become help?*

a _____
b _____

3 Ich mag ihre Einstellung nicht. → *I don't like her employment.*

a _____
b _____

4 Er ist sehr stolz auf das eigene Organisationsvermögen.
→ *He is very proud on the own organization fortune.*

a _____
b _____

5 Ich habe sie gestern auf dem Flur getroffen.
→ *I've met her on the floor yesterday.*

a _____
b _____

b Now give an example of how using a bilingual dictionary helped you to correct one of the incorrect translations. Explain how it helped you. 📝

35 CHALLENGE ▶ Welcoming tourists

Look at these replies from German hotels in response to enquiries about accommodation. Look up the words underlined in the dictionary to find out what makes the texts funny. In **a** write out the meaning of the words underlined. Then in **b** rewrite the sentences in good English, giving the gist of the intended message. Keep it simple.

1 In the close village you can buy jolly memorials for when you <u>pass away</u>.

a _____
b _____

Skills Practice

2 I am amazing diverted by your entreaty for a room. I can offer you a commodious chamber with a balcony imminent to the romantic gorge and hope you will want to <u>drop in</u>.

   a _____
   b _____

3 Having freshly taken over the proprietry of this notorious house, I am wishful that you remove to me your esteemed <u>costume</u>.

   a _____
   b _____

4 <u>Peculiar</u> arrangements for <u>gross</u> parties.

   a _____
   b _____

Source: Charlie Croker, *Løst in Tränslation*. London, Michael O'Mara Books, 2006

▶ S26 Using a grammar book   SB pp. 152–153 ◀

If you keep track of your mistakes in your homework and class tests, you can improve your English by checking the rules a grammar book.

TIP
Use the 'Exercise Finder', WB pp. 102–103, to find exercises to specific grammar themes in this Workbook.

36 Understanding mistakes

Your teacher has highlighted the following grammar errors. <u>Underline</u> the grammatical field involved and use your grammar book to correct the errors, stating the page number or paragraph in your grammar book. Then explain briefly what the mistake is.

1 We **have visited** my exchange partner in Canada last year.
   Error: adjective/adverb • definite article • tense • word order

   Correction: _____

   Explanation: _____
   _____

2 I think **the** Canadian society is fascinating.
   Error: adjective/adverb • definite article • tense • word order

   Correction: _____

   Explanation: _____
   _____

3 We **are learning** English **since** six years.
   Error: adjective/adverb • definite article • tense • word order

   Correction: _____

   Explanation: _____
   _____

4 They spoke too **slow**.
   Error: adjective/adverb • definite article • tense • word order

   Correction: _____

   Explanation: _____
   _____

Skills Practice

S27 • Study skills

▶ S27 Working with visual material SB pp. 153-154 ◀

Visual elements, such as photos, posters or drawings, are powerful tools in helping to explain or illustrate things. Often it is useful or necessary to be able to comment on them.

37 Describing an advert

Source: *Radio Times*, 12 December 2013

a Describe the advertisement above, following the steps listed on SB pp. 153–154.

b Analyse the advert's message. When was it published?

c Evaluate how effective the ad is in achieving its aim. Give your opinion.

S28 • Study skills

▶ S28 Working with charts and graphs SB pp. 154–156

Charts and graphs are used to present detailed information in a clear visual way.

38 Irish GDP vs GNP

Describe the line graph on the right. Use the phrases in the box to help you.

> a sharp decrease • a slight decline • a steady increase •
> (in) both ... and ... • fairly stable • level off • pretty constant

This _____ ¹ deals with the development of the Irish economy between 2000 and 2012. The blue line represents the

_____ ², with the red line showing

_____ ³. Both are closely related. From 2000 to 2007 there is a _____ ⁴ in GNP and GDP, followed from 2007 to 2008 by a _____ ⁵ in both figures. From 2008 to 2009 there is then a _____

_____ ⁶ and GNP. From 2009 onwards both figures _____ ⁷, remaining

_____ ⁸.

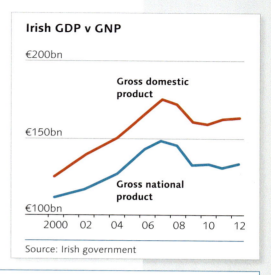

Source: Irish government

TIP

Gross Domestic Product (*Bruttoinlandsprodukt*) is the value of goods sold and services paid for inside a country.

Gross National Product (*Bruttosozialprodukt*) is the value of goods and services in a country including income from other countries.

▶ S29 Working with cartoons SB pp. 156–157

Cartoons are humorous or satirical drawings that often comment on a topical event or issue. You may be asked to describe a cartoon, analyse the point the cartoonist is making and state how effective you find the cartoon.

39 In return for an increase in my allowance, ...

Do the following tasks, using the Language help boxes on SB pp. 156–157.

a Describe the cartoon systematically. What does it show?

_____
_____
_____

"In return for an increase in my allowance, I can offer you free unlimited in-home computer tech support."

b Analyse the cartoon. Does it have a caption? What point is the cartoonist making?

_____
_____
_____
_____
_____

c Evaluate how effective the cartoon is in achieving its aims. Give reasons for your opinion.

Skills Practice

Exam Practice

Verbs for tasks ('Operatoren')

1 What do these verbs mean?

Match the examples of verbs used in context (1–10) with the explanations of what they mean (a–j).

1 <u>Summarize</u> the writer's reasons for supporting the campaign.
2 <u>Write</u> a characterization of the girl and her father.
3 <u>Describe</u> the methods used to prevent oil spills.
4 <u>Outline</u> the author's arguments in favour of going to Mars.
5 <u>Show</u> that you understand why the narrator sympathizes with the woman in the story.
6 <u>Define</u> the use of the word 'sustainably sourced'.
7 <u>Comment on</u> the claim that fracking is an ideal solution to future energy shortages.
8 <u>Discuss</u> the effects of an ageing population on the economic development of the West.
9 <u>State</u> your own views on how to close the gap between rich and poor countries.
10 <u>Justify</u> your conclusions.

a State the nature and/or meaning of something.
b Give the main features etc. of a topic, omitting minor details.
c Specify something clearly.
d Give a concise account of the main points of something.
e Show adequate grounds for decisions or conclusions.
f Describe and examine the way in which the character is presented.
g Make something clear by giving examples.
h State clearly your opinions on the topic in question, supporting your views with evidence.
i Investigate or examine by argument; give reasons for and against.
j Give a detailed account of something.

▶ Verbs for Tasks ('Operatoren'), SB pp. 208–209

1	2	3	4	5	6	7	8	9	10

Reading and writing

2 Fighting deforestation

> Blogpost by **Areeba Hamid** – March 10, 2014 at 16:59
>
> Here's how two different corporations respond to a consumer's very real and very serious concerns …
>
> One makes a clear promise with ambitious time lines; the other continues as if it's business as usual. This is the difference between Mars and Procter & Gamble.
>
> **Today Mars promised to remove forest destruction from all of its products by the end of 2015.**
>
> People like you want their products to be made without the sort of destruction that drives tigers and orang-utans to the edge of extinction. And when you all speak with one voice, this is the result. Mars joins a growing list of companies that are committing to cleaning up their supply chains: Nestle, Unilever, L'Oreal, Ferrero. But this should be a wake up call for the folks at P&G.

Exam Practice • Reading and writing

15 Ever since we revealed how P&G is sourcing dirty palm oil from forest destruction, its spokespeople have offered no real solution. Instead, they have recycled the same old lines about being committed to so-called "sustainability". And with every company that commits to No Deforestation, P&G's "sustainability" policy is looking more and more shaky. As our activists in Indonesia showed today, this is what "sustainability" means for P&G …

20 This morning, a dozen activists unfurled a giant banner in a plantation owned by Musim Mas – a company we identified as a supplier to P&G and involved in ongoing forest and orang-utan habitat clearance. This is not "sustainable" – at least not for the half a million of you who have already called for forest-friendly products.

25 **What should P&G do?**

P&G must join other companies like Nestle, Unilever, Ferrero, L'Oreal and now Mars, which have committed to No Deforestation policies. These companies recognise that the body P&G relies on to certify "sustainably sourced" palm oil – the Roundtable on Sustainable Palm Oil – is not enough.

30 As my colleague in the US, Joao, recently said, blindly trusting the RSPO, like P&G does, is like buying a used car without checking it out first. You might just end up with a lemon. In this case, P&G doesn't even seem to care enough to investigate its own claims.

It's time P&G finally becomes proud sponsors of rainforests and commits
35 **to No Deforestation. Tell P&G you want products like Head & Shoulders to be forest-friendly. Take action here.**

Areeba Hamid is a forest campaigner at Greenpeace International

Source: http://www.greenpeace.org/international/en/news/Blogs/makingwaves/Protect-Paradise/blog/48456/

32 **a lemon** (infml) sth. that is useless because it does not work properly

a **Understanding the text:** After reading the text, tick the correct boxes. In question 4 more than one answer may be correct.

1 The author's criticism is directed at …
   a ☐ Mars.
   b ☐ Proctor & Gamble.
   c ☐ both companies.

2 She is criticizing them for …
   a ☐ buying palm oil from suppliers involved in deforestation.
   b ☐ opposing sustainability.
   c ☐ cutting down forests themselves to plant trees for palm oil.

3 She claims that the spokespeople have …
   a ☐ refused to commit themselves to the principle of sustainability.
   b ☐ said that they support recycling.
   c ☐ simply insisted that they are in favour of sustainability.

4 The author says that they need to …
   a ☐ commit to No Deforestation projects.
   b ☐ drop Musim Mas as their supplier.
   c ☐ plant new forests to provide orang-utans with a new habitat.
   d ☐ stop trusting the RSPO to certify what palm oil is sustainably sourced.
   e ☐ plant lemon trees so that the soil can recover.

E Exam Practice • Reading and writing

b Understanding the text: Now use your answers to **1a** to deal with the tasks below.

1 State which company or companies the author is criticizing and why.
_____
_____

2 Describe what she specifically accuses the spokespeople of doing.
_____
_____

3 Summarize the solution she suggests for the problem.
_____
_____

c Analysing the text: Answer the questions below.

1 State what text type this is. Underline the correct answer.

argumentative – descriptive – expository – persuasive

2 Decide whether the text achieves its purpose. Then analyse the main features which are used to do this. Use the Language help on SB p. 126 to help you.

Purpose of text: _____
_____
_____

Target audience: _____
_____

Expressing attitude – use of adjectives and intensifiers, or typographical devices:
_____
_____
_____

Argumentation – use of colourful adjectives, emotional images, etc.:
_____
_____
_____
_____

Other methods: _____
_____
_____
_____
_____

d Commenting on the text: In your exercise book, comment on the content of the text. Assume that your comment is directed at your fellow students as part of an Environmental Week organized by several European schools, including your own. Write 250–300 words in support of your ideas.

▶ S6: Reading and analysing non-fiction, WB p. 60

■ TIP
Remember that underlining, bold or italic type, colours and different types of font can also be used to highlight aspects which the author regards as important.

▶ S13: The stages of writing, WB pp. 72–73

3 Rise of the open-source coder generation

a Read the following text, then do the tasks on page 96.

1 [...] The 220 clubs that have sprung up worldwide over the last two and a half years started when James Whelton, now 21, saw demand for his after-school meetings teaching HTML and CSS expand beyond the corridors of Presentation Brothers College in Cork.

2 By that stage, the young Irishman had been earning money building websites for local businesses for six years and was the first person in the world to hack a new iPod, in turn building up his reputation among online peers. It was a distant cry from his more solitary early years. "I say to people that some kids have friends when they were growing up, I had keyboards," he said.

"I saw that computing was a very real thing just through the feeling and pure ecstasy of solving a problem, or getting people to visit a website and seeing that it was a sustainable thing.

3 "People heard that I could hack because I had my track record as an academic underachiever and people thought that if that idiot Whelton can programme, then anyone can. I think my friends were interested and we organised a get-together. It was now cool in a lot of people's eyes."

Whelton's online reputation resulted in an invitation to speak at the Dublin Web Summit in 2011, on the same day that he was due to sit his mock final maths exam, where he met Bill Liao, an Australian entrepreneur who wanted to take the classes further.

4 In the summer of 2011, the CoderDojos – named after martial arts training areas or "dojos" – began to spread, around Ireland and then abroad. In the UK there are 37, with 10 in Japan, four in India and one each in Panama, Bolivia, South Africa and Brazil.

5 IT professionals give up their time to help children learn to code, at the same time encouraging the children to eventually become tutors themselves.

The classes are held in universities and company offices empty at weekends – among other venues – in what is called "an open-source, volunteer-led, global movement" where children under the age of 12 have to be accompanied by an adult. Rules are thin on the ground, apart from: "Be Cool – bullying, lying, wasting people's time and so on is uncool."

6 "The idea of a computer club is not new, you are just essentially throwing people in a room and trying to teach them. But what you are teaching them – helping others, being open and transparent – was what defined us," Whelton said.

"There were a lot of philosophies we liked around the dojo – when you go to one you get help, work in teams, practise what you have done, show off what you have done. The more senior you get, the more you mentor young people.

7 "We applied a lot of these logics and principles to a coding club. We thought that if we influenced how we taught kids programming we could get to make more apps that were open source. We could get them to make apps for social causes and for good."

The appetite for the computing dojos grew quickly. The Dublin class was frequently booked up in less than a minute, while word soon spread to Japan and the US, where dojos were also set up.

8 Their success comes from working with a generation of children who have had access to computing since they were a young age, while at the same time not having to adhere to traditional classroom teaching structures, said Whelton. Some of the measurements of the clubs' successes are how previously insular or isolated children come out of their shells in the classes, he said. [...]

Source: Shane Hickey, *The Guardian*, 23 March 2014

E Exam Practice • Reading and writing

▶ S3: Marking up a text, SB pp. 122–123

b Understanding the text: After reading the text say whether the statements below are <u>true</u>, <u>false</u> or you can't say because the information is <u>not in the text</u>. <mark>Highlight</mark> the relevant passage(s) in the text. The first one has been done for you.

	Statement	True	False	Not in text
1	James Whelton had always been good at school.		✔	
2	He started the CoderDojo clubs four years ago.			
3	By 2011 Whelton had been building websites for six years.			
4	He was motivated because he felt very happy about solving problems.			
5	CoderDojos are named after the Director of Japanese Origami, the Great High Dojo.			
6	CoderDojos are run by IT experts who assist children in learning to code.			
7	If there is any bullying, the people taking part should tell the teacher.			
8	The people going to these dojos work strictly on their own; only professional teachers are allowed to teach there.			
9	The aim of the dojos is to prepare students for a job in the computer industry.			
10	They are successful because the young people there have had access to computing for a long time and because they do not use traditional classroom teaching.			
11	One feature of the dojos' success is that children who used to be isolated have now opened up.			

c Analysing the text: Now complete these tasks.

1 State what text type this is. Underline the correct answer. Look at SB pp. 124–125 for help.

   argumentative – descriptive – expository – persuasive

2 Show the structure of the text by matching the headings a–k with paragraphs 1–8. There are three more headings than you need.

   a Anyone can do it
   b Apps for a good cause
   c Beginnings
   d Early expansion
   e From drugs to computers
   f New approach

   g Pupils turn tutors
   h The roots of success
   i The venue is the message
   j Women into computers
   k Worldwide presence

1	2	3	4	5	6	7	8

▶ S6: Reading and analysing non-fiction, WB p. 60

Exam Practice • Listening

Listening

4 Ozone hole history offers climate lesson

a Listening for gist: Listen to the recording once and tick the correct box.
Mario Molina and Sherwood Roland showed the link between …
a ☐ the ozone layer and global population growth.
b ☐ the ozone layer and global warming.
c ☐ the expansion of the ozone layer and the reduction in greenhouse gases.

b Listening for detail: Read the questions, then listen to the recording again. Tick the correct box. (In question 2 more than one answer may be correct.)
1 Mario Molina and Sherwood Roland discovered the harmful effects of …
  a ☐ PVCs in the 1960s.   b ☐ CFCs in the 1970s.   c ☐ DVDs in the 1980s.
2 The substances were contained in …
  a ☐ hair dryers.   b ☐ air conditioners.   c ☐ hair conditioners.
  d ☐ air fresheners.   e ☐ cans of air spray.   f ☐ hair spray canisters.
3 Molina and Roland discovered that these could destroy the …
  a ☐ ozone layer.   b ☐ South Pole.   c ☐ Antarctic ice shelf.
4 Some scientists …
  a ☐ denied that this was true.
  b ☐ lobbied the US government to take action against Molina and Roland.
  c ☐ denied opposing Molina and Roland.
5 The US and the rest of the world crafted the Montreal Protocol …
  a ☐ in 1998.   b ☐ in 1989.   c ☐ in 1999.
6 As a result of the Montreal Protocol …
  a ☐ the ozone layer has fewer holes.
  b ☐ the gap in the ozone layer has become bigger.
  c ☐ the hole in the ozone layer has not got any larger.
7 New research now shows that there is a statistically significant link between the Montreal Protocol and a reduction in …
  a ☐ global warming.
  b ☐ the area of global warming.
  c ☐ the speed of global warming

You can download this audio file and transcript here:

 Webcode starwb-11

▶ S1: Listening for information, WB pp. 56–57

5 'Bottle boards' ride new wave of recycling

a Before listening, try to anticipate what the audio clip is about. Tick the correct box or boxes.

It's probably about …
a ☐ the bottle collection committees which are involved in recycling.
b ☐ re-using old bottles.
c ☐ recycling bottles on board ships to avoid waste.
d ☐ the new fashion for surfing while drinking out of bottles.
e ☐ using surfboards made from recycled bottles.

b Now listen to the recording and complete the notes. The first one has been done for you. The vocabulary box will help you with difficult words. 📝
1 Where? *along Lima's coast (Peru)*
2 Conventional boards made of …
3 Carlos Pino's boards made of …
4 Advantages of Carlos Pino's boards: …
5 Carlos Pino's background: …
6 How are the boards made? …
6 Who is Nadia Balducci? …
8 Nadia's attitude: …

> awareness • director • disposable •
> dry ice • eco-friendly • environmental •
> fibreglass (BE) / fiberglass (AE) • inexpensive •
> lifeguard • plastic pollution • benefit •
> plaster sth. together • (to) practise (BE) /
> practice (AE) • take action

You can download this audio file and transcript here:

 Webcode starwb-12

▶ S1: Listening for information, WB pp. 56–57

Exam Practice • Mediation

Mediation

6 Kölner Tafel e.V.
  a Read the text below about this registered charity active in Cologne.

> **Die Kölner Tafel** ist im Juni 1995 nach dem amerikanischen Vorbild City Harvest und in Anlehnung an bereits in Deutschland bestehende Tafeln als eingetragener, mildtätiger Verein gegründet worden.
>
> Die Kölner Tafel ist mittlerweile zu einer unverzichtbaren sozialen Einrichtung im Kölner Hilfesystem geworden, die es sich zur Aufgabe gemacht hat, Menschen in Not mit dem scheinbar Selbstverständlichsten zu helfen: mit Lebensmitteln, Aufmerksamkeit und mit Solidarität. In Köln sind ausreichend Lebensmittel vorhanden. Ein nicht unerheblicher Prozentsatz wird jedoch täglich vernichtet und zwar nur deshalb, weil Farbe oder Gewicht der Ware den Bestimmungen nicht genügen oder weil zu viel produziert oder eingekauft wurde. Auf der anderen Seite gibt es Menschen, die in Sorge um ihre tägliche Ernährung leben.
>
> Genau hier schaffen die ehrenamtlichen Helfer der Kölner Tafel Abhilfe. Mit Kühltransportern holen sie tonnenweise gespendete Lebensmittel bei Supermärkten, Bäckereien und Herstellern ab. Viele spenden täglich, andere sporadisch. Neue Spender sind immer willkommen.
>
> **Ziel**
>   der Kölner Tafel ist, die Ernährungslage von Bedürftigen in der Stadt Köln zu verbessern.
>
> **Aufgabe**
>   der Kölner Tafel ist, die gespendeten Lebensmittel abzuholen und kostenlos an Einrichtungen im Kölner Hilfesystem weiterzuleiten.
>
> **Ehrenamtliche Helfer**
>   Die Kölner Tafel wird ehrenamtlich von ca. 80 Tafelhelferinnen und -helfern unterstützt.
>
> **Mildtätiger Verein**
>   Die Kölner Tafel ist ein mildtätiger Verein, der sich aus Geld-, Sachspenden und Mitgliedsbeiträgen trägt.
>
> **Leistung**
>   Die Kölner Tafel bewegt jedes Jahr ca. 750 Tonnen Lebensmittel. Dabei legen die 7 Kühlfahrzeuge etwa 110.000 km zurück. (Stand: 2009)
>
> Source: http://www.koelner-tafel.de/01_ueberuns.html

  b Imagine that an American friend who doesn't speak German has asked you about charities that recycle unwanted food in Germany. She needs it for a survey she is doing for her school magazine on ways of helping the poor in different countries.
  First **highlight** the most important points in the German text. Then write a text in English which accurately reflects the main points of the German original. Use the words/phrases in the box to help you.

> *donations of money and goods • manufacturer • membership fee • refrigerated lorry (BE) / refrigerated truck (AE, BE) • registered charity • regularly • conform to regulations*

▶ S21: Mediation of written and oral texts, WB pp. 81–83

Exam Practice • Mediation

7 Globalized people

You want to show Nick, a US high school student on a visit to Germany, your local area. Your mother has asked you to get her some fruit and vegetables from a local shop run by Ahmet Öztürk. Ahmet notices that you are speaking English to Nick and starts up a conversation. Mediate for Ahmet and Nick.

You: Ich bekomme zwei Paprika, vier Zucchini, sechs Kiwi und zwei Mangos, bitte.

Ahmet: Das macht € 8,70. Sie haben einen englischen Freund mit. Kommt er aus London?

You: Er ist kein Engländer, sondern Amerikaner. *(To Nick)* He wants to know where you're from. He thought you were English.

Nick: You can tell him that some of my ancestors were English, but the other half of the family was Irish, and we even have a few Germans in our family tree.

You: _____

Ahmet: Interessant. Bei uns ist es ähnlich. Ein Teil meiner Familie stammt aus Griechenland. Vor dem Ersten Weltkrieg wohnten viele Türken in Griechenland. Ein Onkel von mir wohnt auf Zypern. Er spricht sehr gut Englisch. Wir kommen selbst aus Izmir, an der Westküste der Türkei.

You: He says _____

Nick: I didn't realize there were Turks in Germany until you told me. How long has he been over here?

You: _____

Ahmet: Ach, ich bin schon lange hier. Seit gut zwanzig Jahren. Ich bin mit 1983 mit meiner Frau Başak nach Deutschland gekommen. Ich habe zuerst in der Fabrik gearbeitet, habe viel Geld gespart. Ich habe mir dann das restliche Geld von meinem Cousin geliehen und dieses Geschäft gekauft. Das Geschäft habe ich jetzt seit zwölf Jahren.

You: _____

Nick: Fascinating. It's a bit like the American dream, on a small scale. Tell him that my grandfather started out like that, too. He set up a small store selling candy in the 1940s. The store expanded into a supermarket, then my father bought more stores, and we now own a chain of supermarkets in the Chicago area.

You: _____

Ahmet: Ach, es ist schon halb zwölf. Wir müssen weg. Tschüss, Ahmet, es war sehr interessant!

Nick: Bye. It was really nice talking to you.

Ahmet: Vergessen Sie Ihren Einkauf nicht!

▶ S21: Mediation of written and oral texts, WB pp. 81–83

E

Exam Practice • Speaking (monologue)

Speaking (monologue)

8 Environmental protest

a Make notes on the picture below to complete the following tasks:

1 Describe the picture.

_____
_____
_____

2 Analyse the picture. (What is its aim and how does it achieve this?)

_____
_____
_____
_____

3 Comment on the picture. (Does it achieve its aim?)

_____
_____
_____
_____

b Now describe, analyse and comment on it, using your notes. You should take about two minutes for this task.

Greenpeace activists hold a banner inside palm oil concession owned by PT Multi Persada Gatramegah (PT MPG), a subsidiary of Musim Mas company, a palm oil supplier to Procter and Gamble in Muara Teweh, North Barito, Central Kalimantan. 10/03/2014

Exam Practice • Speaking (dialogue)

9 Cartoon
a Make notes on the cartoon to complete the following tasks. Look at SB pp. 156–157 if you need help.
1 Describe the cartoon.

_____
_____
_____

2 Analyse the cartoon. (How does it achieve its aim?)

_____
_____
_____

3 Comment on the cartoon. (Does it achieve its aim?)

_____
_____
_____

b Now describe, analyse and comment on it, using your notes. You should take about two minutes for this task.

"True, money can't buy happiness, but it can buy cognac, fine cigars and the company of beautiful women, and these make me very happy indeed."

▶ S29: Working with cartoons, WB p. 91

Speaking (dialogue)

10 To gap, or not to gap: that is the question

In your exam you've been asked to discuss with a partner the advantages and disadvantages of a gap year abroad after school, before you start work or go to university. Respond to your partner's remarks, using the cues and adding ideas of your own. Look at SB pp. 162–163 if you need help.

Partner: I don't see the point of spending a whole year abroad after school. I'm not sure yet what I'll do, but I'd rather start a job or go straight to university.

You: | not the way I see it, I'm afraid • useful: broadens horizon |

Partner: OK, there's something in what you say, but what do you mean by 'broadening your horizon'?

You: | see different country • improve foreign language skills • get to know different culture |

Partner: Alright, but I'd rather be earning money or start learning something at university.

You: | another thing • year abroad: looks good on CV • employers, universities like kids • see a bit of the world before start a job or studying • think they're more mature • they're right |

Partner: Oh, I don't agree with that at all. I think that's rubbish. Going abroad for a year is very expensive, and there's no guarantee it'll get you a better job or help you to get a place at university. My brother spent a year in India. He enjoyed it, but he said nobody asked about it when he went to university. All that was important was his grades at Abitur. I don't think he really learned all that much while he was there, either. In fact …

You: | sorry • just stop there for a moment • say he enjoyed it • also important • isn't it? • Abitur pretty stressful • need a break between school and job or uni • have to work hard for both • what's more: work abroad • a stay abroad doesn't have to be expensive |

Partner: Well, I suppose you do have a point there. Maybe I'll think it over.

Exam Practice
101

Exercise Finder

The 'Exercise Finder' helps you to find specific types of exercise, e.g. all the exercises in the WB that practise vocabulary or grammar.

Vocabulary

General
Chapter 1	Ex. 1a, p. 4	Ex. 6, p. 8	Ex. 15a, p. 14
Chapter 2	Ex. 1a, p. 17		
Literature 2	Ex. 4a, p. 29		
Chapter 3	Ex. 7, p. 36	Ex. 8, p. 36	Ex. 9, p. 37
	Ex. 10, p. 37	Ex. 11, p. 38	Ex. 13, p. 39
Chapter 4	Ex. 1, p. 43	Ex. 4, p. 46	Ex. 14, p. 52

Collocations
Chapter 1	Ex. 2, p. 7	Ex. 4, p. 7	
Chapter 2	Ex. 3, p. 20	Ex. 4, p. 20	Ex. 5, p. 20
Chapter 3	Ex. 2, p. 30	Ex. 7, p. 36	Ex. 8, p. 36
	Ex. 9, p. 37	Ex. 10, p. 37	Ex. 11, p. 38
	Ex. 13, p. 39		
Chapter 4	Ex. 1, p. 43	Ex. 4, p. 46	Ex. 14, p. 52

Pronunciation
Chapter 1	Ex. 3, p. 7	Ex. 8, p. 9

Word building
Chapter 3	Ex. 2a, p. 30

Grammar

Active/passive
Skill 19	Ex. 26b, p. 79

Adjectives/adverbs
Chapter 2	Ex. 9, p. 24

Apostrophes
Chapter 3	Ex. 16, p. 40

Finding/correcting mistakes
Chapter 2	Ex. 12, p. 25	
Chapter 4	Ex. 6, p. 47	Ex. 13, p. 51
Skill 26	Ex. 36, p. 89	

Indirect speech
Chapter 1	Ex. 13, p. 13

Modal verbs
Chapter 2	Ex. 11, p. 25

Prepositions
Chapter 3	Ex. 1, p. 30

Tenses
Chapter 1	Ex. 7, p. 9		
Chapter 2	Ex. 12, p. 25	Ex. 13, p. 26	Ex. 14, p. 26
	Ex. 15, p. 27		
Chapter 3	Ex. 12, p. 38		
Chapter 4	Ex. 6, p. 47	Ex. 14, p. 52	

Verb + gerund / to-infinitive
Chapter 1	Ex. 9, p. 10

Writing

Comments/analysis (cf. also Skill 17)
Chapter 1	Ex. 1b, p. 4	Ex. 10b, p. 11	Ex. 11, p. 11
Chapter 2	Ex. 1b, p. 17	Ex. 6c, p. 21	
Chapter 4	Ex. 9, p. 49		
Literature 4	Ex. 3b, p. 55		
Skill 6	Ex. 4d, p. 60		
Skill 7	Ex. 6a, p. 61	Ex. 6b, p. 62	Ex. 7d, p. 63
	Ex. 8c, p. 63		
Skill 9	Ex. 15c, p. 68		
Skill 27	Ex. 37c, p. 90		
Exam Practice	Ex. 2d, p. 94		

Creative writing (cf. Skill 14)

Skills

Skill 1: Listening for information (Exs. 1–2, pp. 56–57)
Chapter 1	Ex. 5, p. 8	
Chapter 2	Ex. 8, p. 23	
Chapter 3	Ex. 6, p. 35	
Chapter 4	Ex. 7a, p. 47	Ex. 7b, p. 48
Exam Practice	Ex. 4, p. 97	Ex. 5, p. 97

Skill 2: Viewing a film
Chapter 4	Ex. 12, p. 51

Skill 3: Marking up a text (p. 57)
Chapter 2	Ex. 16, p. 27	
Skill 7	Ex. 5a, p. 61	
Skill 9	Ex. 14a, p. 68	
Skill 17	Ex. 24a, p. 76	
Skill 18	Ex. 25a, p. 77	
Skill 20	Ex. 27a, p. 79	
Skill 21	Ex. 28, p. 81	Ex. 29, p. 83

Skill 4: Skimming and scanning
Chapter 4	Ex. 12, p. 51		
Skill 5	Ex. 3, pp. 58–59		
Skill 6	Ex. 4a, p. 60		
Skill 7	Ex. 5a, p. 61	Ex. 7a, p. 62	Ex. 8a, p. 63
Skill 9	Ex. 9a, pp. 64–65		

Skill 5: Identifying text types (Ex. 3, pp. 58–59)
Skill 6	Ex. 4a, p. 60	
Exam Practice	Ex. 2c, p. 94	Ex. 3c, p. 96

Skill 6: Reading and analysing non-fiction (Ex. 4, p. 60)
Chapter 2	Ex. 16, p. 27	
Chapter 3	Ex. 15, p. 40	
Chapter 4	Ex. 12, p. 51	
Skill 5	Ex. 3, pp. 58–59	
Exam Practice	Ex. 2, pp. 92–94	Ex. 3, pp. 95–96

Exercise Finder

Skill 7: Reading and analysing narrative prose (Exs. 5–8, pp. 61–63)			
Chapter 1	Ex. 10, p. 11		
Literature 1	Ex. 1, p. 15	Ex. 2, p. 16	Ex. 3, p. 16
Literature 2	Ex. 1, p. 28	Ex. 2, p. 28	Ex. 3, p. 29
	Ex. 4, p. 29		

Skill 8: Reading, watching and analysing drama (Exs. 9–11, pp. 64–66)			
Literature 4	Ex. 1, p. 54	Ex. 2, p. 55	Ex. 3, p. 55

Skill 9: Reading and analysing poetry (Exs. 12–15, pp. 66–68)			
Literature 3	Ex. 1, p. 41	Ex. 2, p. 41	Ex. 3, p. 42
Chapter 4	Ex. 4b, p. 51		

Skill 10: Giving a presentation (Ex. 16, p. 69)	
Chapter 1	Ex. 14, p. 14

Skill 11: Communicating in everyday situations (Ex. 17, pp. 70–71)	

Skill 12: Having a discussion (Ex. 18, pp. 71–72)	
Exam Practice	Ex. 10, p. 101

Skill 13: The stages of writing (Ex. 19, pp. 72–73)			
Chapter 1	Ex. 1b, p. 4	Ex. 11, p. 11	Ex. 15b, p. 14
Chapter 2	Ex. 1b, p. 17	Ex. 6c, p. 21	Ex. 7, p. 22
Chapter 3	Ex. 15, p. 40		
Chapter 4	Ex. 9, p. 49		
Skill 17	Ex. 24c, pp. 76–77		
Skill 20	Ex. 27c, p. 81		

Skill 14: Creative writing (Ex. 20, pp. 73–74)		
Chapter 1	Ex. 1a, p. 4	Ex. 15b, p. 14
Literature 1	Ex. 4c, p. 29	
Literature 2	Ex. 4, p. 29	
Chapter 3	Ex. 11b, p. 37	Ex. 14, p. 39
Chapter 4	Ex. 10, p. 50	Ex. 14, p. 52

Skill 15: Writing a formal letter or email (Ex. 21, p. 74)	
Chapter 1	Ex. 13b, p. 13
Literature 1	Ex. 3b, p. 16
Chapter 3	Ex. 10, p. 37
Chapter 4	Ex. 10, p. 50

Skill 16: Writing an application (Exs. 22–23, pp. 75–76)

Skill 17: Argumentative writing (Ex. 24, pp. 76–77)
cf. also Writing: comments/analysis

Skill 18: Writing a review (Ex. 25, pp. 77–78)

Skill 19: Writing a report (Ex. 26, pp. 78–79)

Skill 20: Writing a summary (Ex. 27, pp. 79–81)		
Skill 6	Ex. 4b, p. 60	
Skill 8	Ex. 9b, p. 65	
Skill 21	Ex. 28 pp. 81–82	Ex. 29, p. 83

Skill 21: Mediation of written and oral texts (Exs. 28–29, pp. 81–83)	
Chapter 2	Ex. 16, p. 27
Chapter 3	Ex. 5 pp. 34–35

Chapter 4	Ex. 15, p. 53		
Exam Practice	Ex. 6, p. 98	Ex. 7, p. 99	

Skill 22: Making and taking notes (Ex. 30, p. 84)		
Literature 1	Ex. 1a, p. 15	
Chapter 2	Ex. 8c, p. 23	
Chapter 3	Ex. 6, p. 35	
Skill 1	Ex. 2b, p. 57	
Skill 7	Ex. 5a, p. 61	Ex. 7a, p. 62
Skill 8	Ex. 9a, p. 64	
Skill 9	Ex. 12, pp. 66–67	
Skill 16	Ex. 22a, p. 75	
Skill 17	Ex. 24b, pp. 76–77	
Skill 20	Ex. 27b, pp. 79–81	

Skill 23: Dealing with unknown words (Ex. 31, pp. 84–85)			
Literature 1	Ex. 1, p. 15	Ex. 3, p. 16	
Chapter 2	Ex. 8, p. 23		
Skill 6	Ex. 4, p. 60		
Skill 7	Ex. 5, p. 61	Ex. 7, p. 62	Ex. 8, p. 63
Skill 9	Ex. 12, pp. 66–67		
Skill 17	Ex. 24a, p. 76		
Skill 20	Ex. 27a, pp. 79–80		
Skill 21	Ex. 29, p. 83		
cf. also Skill 25			

Skill 24: Learning new words
cf. Vocabulary

Skill 25: Using a dictionary (Exs. 32–35, pp. 86–89)
Chapter 1	Ex. 12, p. 12
cf. also Skill 23

Skill 26: Using a grammar book (Ex. 36, p. 89)
cf. also Grammar

Skill 27: Working with visual material (Ex. 37, p. 90)
Exam Practice	Ex. 8, p. 100

Skill 28: Working with charts and graphs (Ex. 38, p. 91)
Chapter 2	Ex. 10, p. 24
Chapter 4	Ex. 2, p. 43

Skill 29: Working with cartoons (Ex. 39, p. 91)
Chapter 2	Ex. 6, p. 21
Exam Practice	Ex. 9, p. 101

Skill 31: Using search engines (Ex. 40, p. 92)

Exam Practice
Verbs for tasks ('Operatoren') (Ex. 1, p. 92)
Reading and writing (Exs. 2–3, pp. 92–96)
Listening (Exs. 4–5, p. 97)
Mediation (Exs. 6–7, pp. 98–99)
Speaking (monologue) (Exs. 8–9, pp. 100–101)
Speaking (dialogue) (Ex. 10, p. 101)

Acknowledgements

Texts

p. 12: Cornelsen/Oxford University Press 2009; **pp. 15-16:** © Kevin Brooks, 2010; **p. 28:** © Alice Munro, 2012; **p. 29:** © Guardian News & Media Ltd 2012; **p. 41:** © Roger McGough, 2002; **pp. 54-55:** © 1986 by Alfred Uhry; **pp. 58-59:** © Guardian News & Media Ltd., 2013; **p. 60:** © 2011 Freakonomics, LLC. All rights reserved; **pp. 61-63:** © Bill Barich, 1982, reprinted by permission of Darhansoff & Verrill, New York; **pp. 64-65:** © Paven Virk, 2012; **p. 80:** © Guardian News & Media Ltd. 2013; **p. 82:** Jens-Peter Marquardt/ARD aktuell/Tagesschau.de; **p. 83:** © Tom McArthur/Oxford University Press, 2012; **p. 84:** © Natasha Solomons, 2010; **p. 86:** Oxford University Press; **p. 93:** © Areeba Hamid/Greenpeace International; **p. 95:** © Guardian News & Media Ltd 2014; **p. 98:** Kölner Tafel e.V./www.koelner-tafel.de; **Answer Key & Transcripts: pp. 1-2:** Guardian News & Media Ltd 2013; **pp. 8-10:** Guardian News & Media Ltd 2013; **pp. 14-15:** Reprinted with permission – Torstar Syndication Services; **pp. 18-19:** © http://wlacademicyearprograms.tumblr.com/; **pp. 23-24:** The Economist Newspaper Limited, London; **pp. 39-40:** ITN Source/Reuters.

Photos/Illustrations

p. 4: top: oliveromg/Shutterstock, bottom: Cultura RF/vario images; **p. 7:** wavebreakmedia/Shutterstock; **p. 8:** AVAVA/Shutterstock; **p. 10:** Everett Collection/Shutterstock; **p. 11:** picture alliance/Neil Emmerson; **p. 13:** © JLP/Jose Luis Pelaez/Corbis; **p. 14:** Christian Schwier/Fotolia; **p. 15:** Cornelsen Schulverlage (photo: © Rupert Warren/Plainpicture); **p. 17:** top: Angela Waye/Shutterstock, bottom: Image Source/vario images; **p. 20:** © Chris Rout/Alamy/mauritius images; **p. 21:** left: © Nick Baker/Reproduced by kind permission of PRIVATE EYE magazine www.private-eye.co.uk, right: © Simon Key/Reproduces by kind permission of PRIVATE EYE magazine www.private-eye.co.uk; **p. 22:** nenetus/Shutterstock; **p. 27:** © mark phillips/Alamy/mauritius images; **p. 28:** ZUMAPRESS.com/dpa/picture alliance; **p. 29:** © Jill Mayhew/Capital Pictures/United Archives/mauritius images; **p. 30:** indianstockimages/Shutterstock; **p. 33:** © Frans Lanting/Mint Images RM/vario images; **p. 34:** TheFinalMiracle/Shutterstock; **p. 35:** © Liba Taylor/R/dpa/picture alliance; **p. 37:** Jasmin Awad/Shutterstock; **p. 39:** Loop Images/vario images; **p. 42:** Your_Photo_Today/A1Pix; **p. 43:** Poznyakov/Shutterstock; **p. 47:** Goodluz/Shutterstock; **p. 48:** Hannamariah/Shutterstock; **p. 49:** girl: hartphotography/Shutterstock, Melbourne skyline: Gordon Bell/Shutterstock; **p. 50:** Roland Beier, Berlin; **p. 52:** left: auremar/Shutterstock, middle: All Canada Photos/dpa/picture alliance, top right: Olesia Bilkei/Shutterstock, bottom right: oliveromg/Shutterstock; **p. 53:** © Ben Welsh/Corbis; **p. 60:** karen roach/Shutterstock; **p. 63:** © Larry Lee Photography/Corbis; **p. 67:** © Chris Clor/Blend Images/Corbis; **p. 69:** Image Source/vario images; **p. 70:** Luminis/Shutterstock; **p. 73:** photo: Filip Fuxa/Shutterstock, map: Carlos Borrell, Berlin; **p. 75:** Menna/Shutterstock; **p. 78:** © Tolga Akmen/Anadolu Agency/dpa/picture alliance; **p. 82:** Loop Images/vario images; **p. 90:** © Greenpeace; **p. 91:** © Aaron Bacall/CartoonStock.com; **p. 100:** © Ulet Ifansasti/Greenpeace; **p. 101:** © Tim O'Brien/CartoonStock.com.

Cover: gary 718/Shutterstock